# BIBLE STORYBOOK

*A Collection of Favorite Stories
from the Bible*

This is a Portion of Holy Scripture in the *Contemporary English Version*. The American Bible Society is a not-for-profit organization which publishes the Scriptures without doctrincal note or comment. Since 1816, its single mission has been to make the Word of God easily available to people everywhere at the lowest possible cost and in the languages they understand best. Working toward this goal, the ABS is a member of the United Bible Societies, a worldwide effort that extends to more than 180 countries and territories. You are urged to read the Bible and to share it with others. For a free catalog of Scripture publications, call the American Bible Society at 1-800-32-BIBLE, or write to 1865 Broadway, New York, NY 10023-7505.

Visit the ABS website! **www.americanbible.org.**

Illustrated by
ESBEN HANEFELT KRISTENSEN

ISBN 1-58516-050-4

Printed in Denmark
Eng. Port. CEV560P-107890
ABS-11/99-5,000 — DBS1

# BIBLE STORYBOOK

*A Collection of Favorite Stories
from the Bible*

Contemporary English Version

AMERICAN BIBLE SOCIETY
NEW YORK

# Contents

## Old Testament

# New Testament

*Old Testament*

# The Beginning

## God Creates the World

Genesis
1.1-25

In the beginning God created the heavens and the earth.
The earth was barren, with no form of life;
it was under a roaring ocean covered with darkness.
But the Spirit of God was moving over the water.

### The First Day

God said, "I command light to shine!" And light started shining. God looked at the light and saw that it was good. He separated light from darkness and named the light "Day" and the darkness "Night." Evening came and then morning—that was the first day.

### The Second Day

God said, "I command a dome to separate the water above it from the water below it." And that's what happened. God made the dome and named it "Sky." Evening came and then morning—that was the second day.

### The Third Day

God said, "I command the water under the sky to come together in one place, so there will be dry ground." And that's what happened. God named the dry ground "Land," and he named the water "Ocean." God looked at what he had done and saw that it was good.

God said, "I command the earth to produce all kinds of plants, including fruit trees and grain." And that's what happened. The earth produced all kinds of vegetation. God looked at what he had done, and it was good. Evening came and then morning—that was the third day.

Genesis
3.1-21

### The Fourth Day

God said, "I command lights to appear in the sky and to separate day from night and to show the time for seasons, special days, and years. I command them to shine on the earth." And that's what happened. God made two powerful lights, the brighter one to rule the day and the other to rule the night. He also made the stars. Then God put these lights in the sky to shine on the earth, to rule day and night, and to separate light from darkness. God looked at what he had done, and it was good. Evening came and then morning—that was the fourth day.

### The Fifth Day

God said, "I command the ocean to be full of living creatures, and I command birds to fly above the earth." So God made the giant sea monsters and all the living creatures that swim in the ocean. He also made every kind of bird. God looked at what he had done, and it was good. Then he gave the living creatures his blessing—he told the ocean creatures to live everywhere in the ocean and the birds to live everywhere on earth. Evening came and then morning—that was the fifth day.

### The Sixth Day

God said, "I command the earth to give life to all kinds of tame animals, wild animals, and reptiles." And that's what happened. God made every one of them. Then he looked at what he had done, and it was good.

## God Creates People

Genesis
1.26-28,31

God said, "Now we will make humans, and they will be like us. We will let them rule the fish, the birds, and all other living creatures."

So God created humans to be like himself; he made men and women. God gave them his blessing and said:

> Have a lot of children! Fill the earth with people and bring it under your control. Rule over the fish in the ocean, the birds in the sky, and every animal on the earth. . . .

God looked at what he had done. All of it was very good! Evening came and then morning—that was the sixth day.

Genesis
2.1-4a

So the heavens and the earth and everything else were created.

### The Seventh Day

By the seventh day God had finished his work, and so he rested. God blessed the seventh day and made it special because on that day he rested from his work.

That's how God created the heavens and the earth.

# People Disobey God

## *People in the Garden of Eden*

Genesis
2.4b-9
When the LORD God made the heavens and the earth, no grass or plants were growing anywhere. God had not yet sent any rain, and there was no one to work the land. But streams came up from the ground and watered the earth.

The LORD God took a handful of soil and made a man. God breathed life into the man, and the man started breathing. The LORD made a garden in a place called Eden, which was in the east, and he put the man there.

The LORD God placed all kinds of beautiful trees and fruit trees in the garden. Two other trees were in the middle of the garden. One of the trees gave life—the other gave the power to know the difference between right and wrong.

Genesis
2.15-25
The LORD God put the man in the Garden of Eden to take care of it and to look after it. But the LORD told him, "You may eat fruit from any tree in the garden, except the one that has the power to let you know the difference between right and wrong. If you eat any fruit from that tree, you will die before the day is over!"

The LORD God said, "It isn't good for the man to live alone. I need to make a suitable partner for him." So the LORD took some soil and made animals and birds. He brought them to the man to see what names he would give each of them. Then the man named the tame animals and the birds and the wild animals. That's how they got their names.

None of these was the right kind of partner for the man. So the LORD God made him fall into a deep sleep, and he took out one of the man's ribs. Then after closing the man's side, the LORD made a woman out of the rib.

11

The LORD God brought her to the man, and the man exclaimed,

"Here is someone like me! She is part of my body,
my own flesh and bones. She came from me, a man.
So I will name her Woman!"

That's why a man will leave his own father and mother. He marries a woman, and the two of them become like one person.

Although the man and his wife were both naked, they were not ashamed.

## *People Break God's Command*

The snake was sneakier than any of the other wild animals that the LORD God had made. One day it came to the woman and asked, "Did God tell you not to eat fruit from any tree in the garden?"

The woman answered, "God said we could eat fruit from any tree in the garden, except the one in the middle. He told us not to eat fruit from that tree or even to touch it. If we do, we will die."

"No, you won't!" the snake replied. "God understands what will happen on the day you eat fruit from that tree. You will see what you have done, and you will know the difference between right and wrong, just as God does."

The woman stared at the fruit. It looked beautiful and tasty. She wanted the wisdom that it would give her, and she ate some of the fruit. Her husband was there with her, so she gave some to him, and he ate it too. Right away they saw what they had done, and they realized they were naked. Then they sewed fig leaves together to make something to cover themselves.

Late in the afternoon a breeze began to blow, and the man and woman heard the LORD God walking in the garden. They were frightened and hid behind some trees.

The LORD called out to the man and asked, "Where are you?"

The man answered, "I was naked, and when I heard you walking through the garden, I was frightened and hid!"

"How did you know you were naked?" God asked. "Did you eat any fruit from that tree in the middle of the garden?"

"It was the woman you put here with me," the man said. "She gave me some of the fruit, and I ate it."

The LORD God then asked the woman, "What have you done?"

"The snake tricked me," she answered. "And I ate some of that fruit."

So the LORD God said to the snake:

"Because of what you have done,
    you will be the only animal to suffer this curse—
For as long as you live,
    you will crawl on your stomach and eat dirt.
You and this woman will hate each other;
    your descendants and hers will always be enemies.
One of hers will strike you on the head,
    and you will strike him on the heel."

Then the LORD said to the woman,
"You will suffer terribly when you give birth.
But you will still desire your husband,
    and he will rule over you."

The LORD said to the man,
"You listened to your wife and ate fruit from that tree.
And so, the ground will be under a curse
    because of what you did.
As long as you live, you will have to struggle
    to grow enough food.

13

Your food will be plants, but the ground
    will produce thorns and thistles.
You will have to sweat to earn a living;
you were made out of soil,
    and you will once again turn into soil."

The man Adam named his wife Eve because she would become the mother of all who live.

Then the LORD God made clothes out of animal skins for the man and his wife.

## God Drives People out of Eden

Genesis
3.22-24

The LORD said, "These people now know the difference between right and wrong, just as we do. But they must not be allowed to eat fruit from the tree that lets them live forever." So the LORD God sent them out of the Garden of Eden, where they would have to work the ground from which the man had been made. Then God put winged creatures at the entrance to the garden and a flaming, flashing sword to guard the way to the life-giving tree.

## Cain and Abel

Genesis
4.3-16

Adam and Eve had two sons. The first one, Cain, became a farmer and the second son, Abel, became a shepherd. One day, Cain gave part of his harvest to the LORD, and Abel also gave an offering to the LORD. He killed the first-born lamb from one of his sheep and gave the LORD the best parts of it. The LORD was pleased with Abel and his offering, but not with Cain and his offering. This made Cain so angry that he could not hide his feelings.

The LORD said to Cain:

    What's wrong with you? Why do you have such an angry look on your face? If you had done the right thing, you would be smiling. But you did the wrong thing, and now sin is waiting to attack you like a lion. Sin wants to destroy you, but don't let it!

Cain said to his brother Abel, "Let's go for a walk." And when they were out in a field, Cain killed him.

Afterwards the LORD asked Cain, "Where is Abel?"

"How should I know?" he answered. "Am I supposed to look after my brother?"

Then the LORD said:

Why have you done this terrible thing? You killed your own brother, and his blood flowed onto the ground. Now his blood is calling out for me to punish you. And so, I'll put you under a curse. Because you killed Abel and made his blood run out on the ground, you will never be able to farm the land again. If you try to farm the land, it won't produce anything for you. From now on, you'll be without a home, and you'll spend the rest of your life wandering from place to place.

"This punishment is too hard!" Cain said. "You're making me leave my home and live far from you. I will have to wander about without a home, and just anyone could kill me."

"No!" the LORD answered. "Anyone who kills you will be punished seven times worse than I am punishing you." So the LORD put a mark on Cain to warn everyone not to kill him. But Cain had to go far from the LORD and live in the Land of Wandering, which is east of Eden.

## Noah's Ark

Genesis
6.1,9b-22

More and more people were born, until finally they spread all over the earth . . . .

Noah was the only person who lived right and obeyed God. He had three sons: Shem, Ham, and Japheth.

God knew that everyone was terribly cruel and violent. So he told Noah:

Cruelty and violence have spread everywhere. Now I'm going to destroy the whole earth and all its people. Get some good lumber and build a boat. Put rooms in it and cover it with tar inside and out. Make it four hundred fifty feet long, seventy-five feet wide, and forty-five feet high. Build a roof on the boat and leave a space of about eighteen inches between the roof and the

sides. Make the boat three stories high and put a door on one side.

I'm going to send a flood that will destroy everything that breathes! Nothing will be left alive. But I solemnly promise that you, your wife, your sons, and your daughters-in-law will be kept safe in the boat.

Bring into the boat with you a male and a female of every kind of animal and bird, as well as a male and a female of every reptile. I don't want them to be destroyed. Store up enough food both for yourself and for them.

Noah did everything the LORD told him to do.

## The Flood

Genesis
7.1

The LORD told Noah:

Take your whole family with you into the boat, because you are the only one on this earth who pleases me.

Genesis
7.11-20

Noah was six hundred years old when the water under the earth started gushing out everywhere. The sky opened like windows, and rain poured down for forty days and nights. All this began on the seventeenth day of the second month of the year. On that day Noah and his wife went into the boat with their three sons, Shem, Ham, and Japheth, and their wives. They took along every kind of animal, tame and wild, including the birds. Noah took a male and a female of every living creature with him, just as God had told him to do. And when they were all in the boat, God closed the door.

For forty days the rain poured down without stopping. And the water became deeper and deeper, until the boat started floating high above the ground. Finally, the mighty flood was so deep that even the highest mountain peaks were almost twenty-five feet below the surface of the water.

Genesis
7.22-24

The LORD destroyed everything that breathed. Nothing was left alive except Noah and the others in the boat. A hundred fifty days later, the water started going down.

God did not forget about Noah and the animals with him in the boat. So God made a wind blow, and the water started going down. God stopped up the places where the water had been gushing out from under the earth. He also closed up the sky, and the rain stopped. For one hundred fifty days the water slowly went down. Then on the seventeenth day of the seventh month of the year, the boat came to rest somewhere in the Ararat mountains. The water kept going down, and the mountain tops could be seen on the first day of the tenth month.

Forty days later Noah opened a window to send out a raven, but it kept flying around until the water had dried up. Noah wanted to find out if the water had gone down, and he sent out a dove. Deep water was still everywhere, and the dove could not find a place to land. So it flew back to the boat. Noah held out his hand and helped it back in.

Seven days later Noah sent the dove out again. It returned in the evening, holding in its beak a green leaf from an olive tree. Noah knew that the water was finally going down. He waited seven more days before sending the dove out again, and this time it did not return.

Noah was now six hundred one years old. And by the first day of that year, almost all the water had gone away. Noah made an opening in the roof of the boat and saw that the ground was getting dry. By the twenty-seventh day of the second month, the earth was completely dry.

God said to Noah, "You, your wife, your sons, and your daughters-in-law may now leave the boat. Let out the birds, animals, and reptiles, so they can mate and live all over the earth." After Noah and his family had gone out of the boat, the living creatures left in groups of their own kind.

Noah built an altar where he could offer sacrifices to the LORD. Then he offered on the altar one of each kind of animal and bird that could be used for a sacrifice. The smell of the burning offering pleased God, and he said:

> Never again will I punish the earth for the sinful things its people do. All of them have evil thoughts from the time they are

young, but I will never destroy everything that breathes, as I did this time.

As long as the earth remains,
there will be planting
  and harvest,
    cold and heat;
winter and summer,
  day and night.

## God's Agreement with Noah

Genesis
9.8-17

Again, God said to Noah and his sons:

I am going to make a solemn promise to you and to everyone who will live after you. This includes the birds and the animals that came out of the boat. I promise every living creature that the earth and those living on it will never again be destroyed by a flood.

The rainbow that I have put in the sky will be my sign to you and to every living creature on earth. It will remind you that I will keep this promise forever. When I send clouds over the earth, and a rainbow appears in the sky, I will remember my promise to you and to all other living creatures. Never again will I let floodwaters destroy all life. When I see the rainbow in the sky, I will always remember the promise that I have made to every living creature. The rainbow will be the sign of that solemn promise.

## The Tower of Babel

Genesis
11.1-9

After the flood, Noah's sons had many children. At first everyone spoke the same language, but after some of them moved from the east and settled in Babylonia, they said:

Let's build a city with a tower that reaches to the sky! We'll use hard bricks and tar instead of stone and mortar. We'll become famous, and we won't be scattered all over the world.

But when the LORD came down to look at the city and the tower, he said:

These people are working together because they all speak the same language. This is just the beginning. Soon they will be able to do anything they want. Come on! Let's go down and confuse them by making them speak different languages—then they won't be able to understand each other.

So the people had to stop building the city, because the LORD confused their language and scattered them all over the earth. That's how the city of Babel got its name.

# Abraham and Sarah

## *God Calls and Blesses Abram*

One of Noah's descendants was Terah.

Genesis
11.26-32
After Terah was seventy years old, he had three sons: Abram, Nahor, and Haran, who became the father of Lot. Terah's sons were born in the city of Ur in Chaldea, and Haran died there before the death of his father. The following is the story of Terah's descendants.

Abram married Sarai, but she was not able to have any children. And Nahor married Milcah, who was the daughter of Haran and the sister of Iscah.

Terah decided to move from Ur to the land of Canaan. He took along Abram and Sarai and his grandson Lot, the son of Haran. But when they came to the city of Haran, they decided to settle there instead. Terah lived to be two hundred five years old and died in Haran.

Genesis
12.1-7
The LORD said to Abram:

Leave your country, your family, and your relatives and go to the land that I will show you. I will bless you and make your descendants into a great nation. You will become famous and be a

blessing to others. I will bless anyone who blesses you, but I will put a curse on anyone who puts a curse on you. Everyone on earth will be blessed because of you.

Abram was seventy-five years old when the LORD told him to leave the city of Haran. He obeyed and left with his wife Sarai, his nephew Lot, and all the possessions and slaves they had gotten while in Haran.

When they came to the land of Canaan, Abram went as far as the sacred tree of Moreh in a place called Shechem. The Canaanites were still living in the land at that time, but the LORD appeared to Abram and promised, "I will give this land to your family forever." Abram then built an altar there for the LORD.

## Abram and Lot Separate

During a famine in the country, Abram moved to Egypt and lived there as a foreigner for a while. He then moved back from Egypt to the southern part of the country with his wife and everything that he owned. Abram was very rich with cattle, silver and gold.

Genesis
13.5-13

Lot, who was traveling with Abram, also had sheep, goats, and cattle, as well as his own family and slaves. At this time the Canaanites and the Perizzites were living in the same area, and so there wasn't enough pastureland left for Abram and Lot with all of their animals. Besides this, the men who took care of Abram's animals and the ones who took care of Lot's animals started quarreling.

Abram said to Lot, "We are close relatives. We shouldn't argue, and our men shouldn't be fighting one another. There is plenty of land for you to choose from. Let's separate. If you go north, I'll go south; if you go south, I'll go north."

This happened before the LORD had destroyed the cities of Sodom and Gomorrah. And when Lot looked around, he saw there was plenty of water in the Jordan Valley. All the way to Zoar the valley was as green as the garden of the LORD or the land of Egypt. So Lot chose the whole Jordan Valley for himself, and as he started toward the east, he and Abram separated. Abram stayed in the land of Canaan. But Lot settled near the cities of the valley and put up his tents not far from Sodom, where the people were evil and sinned terribly against the LORD.

## The LORD's Promise to Abram

Genesis
15.1-6

Later the LORD spoke to Abram in a vision, "Abram, don't be afraid! I will protect you and reward you greatly."

But Abram answered, "LORD All-Powerful, you have given me everything I could ask for, except children. And when I die, Eliezer of Damascus will get all I own. You have not given me any children, and this servant of mine will inherit everything."

The LORD replied, "No, he won't! You will have a son of your own, and everything you have will be his." Then the LORD took Abram outside and said, "Look at the sky and see if you can count the stars. That's how many descendants you will have." Abram believed the LORD, and the LORD was pleased with him.

Genesis
17.3-5

Abram bowed with his face to the ground, and God said:

I promise that you will be the father of many nations. That's why I now change your name from Abram to Abraham.

## The LORD Visits Abraham and Sarah

Genesis
18.1-14

One hot summer afternoon Abraham was sitting by the entrance to his tent near the sacred trees of Mamre, when the LORD appeared to him. Abraham looked up and saw three men standing nearby. He quickly ran to meet them, bowed with his face to the ground, and said, "Please come to my home where I can serve you. I'll have some water brought, so you can wash your feet, then you can rest under the tree. Let me get you some food to give you strength before you leave. I would be honored to serve you."

"Thank you very much," they answered. "We accept your offer."

Abraham quickly went to his tent and said to Sarah, "Hurry! Get a large sack of flour and make some bread." After saying this, he rushed off to his herd of cattle and picked out one of the best calves, which his servant quickly prepared. He then served his guests some yogurt and milk together with the meat.

While they were eating, he stood near them under the trees, and they asked, "Where is your wife Sarah?"

"She is right there in the tent," Abraham answered.

One of the guests was the LORD, and he said, "I'll come back about this time next year, and when I do, Sarah will already have a son."

Sarah was behind Abraham, listening at the entrance to the tent. Abraham and Sarah were very old, and Sarah was well past the age for having children. So she laughed and said to herself, "Now that I am worn out and my husband is old, will I really know such happiness?"

The LORD asked Abraham, "Why did Sarah laugh? Does she doubt that she can have a child in her old age? I am the LORD! There is nothing too difficult for me. I'll come back next year at the time I promised, and Sarah will already have a son."

## Abraham Prays for Sodom

Genesis
18.16-33

When the three men got ready to leave, they looked down toward Sodom, and Abraham walked part of the way with them.

The LORD said to himself, "I should tell Abraham what I am going to do, since his family will become a great and powerful nation that will be a blessing to all other nations on earth. I have chosen him to teach his family to obey me forever and to do what is right and fair. Then I will give Abraham many descendants, just as I promised."

The LORD said, "Abraham, I have heard that the people of Sodom and Gomorrah are doing all kinds of evil things. Now I am going down to see for myself if those people really are that bad. If they aren't, I want to know about it."

The men turned and started toward Sodom. But the LORD stayed with Abraham, who asked, "LORD, when you destroy the evil people, are you also going to destroy those who are good? Wouldn't you spare the city if there are only fifty good people in it? You surely wouldn't let them be killed when you destroy the evil ones. You are the judge of all the earth, and you do what is right."

The LORD replied, "If I find fifty good people in Sodom, I will save the city to keep them from being killed."

Abraham answered, "I am nothing more than the dust of the earth. Please forgive me, LORD, for daring to speak to you like this. But suppose there are only forty-five good people in Sodom. Would you still wipe out the whole city?"

"If I find forty-five good people," the LORD replied, "I won't destroy the city."

"Suppose there are just forty good people?" Abraham asked.

"Even for them," the LORD replied, "I won't destroy the city."

Abraham said, "Please don't be angry, LORD, if I ask you what you will do if there are only thirty good people in the city."

"If I find thirty," the LORD replied, "I still won't destroy it."

Then Abraham said, "I don't have any right to ask you, LORD, but what would you do if you find only twenty?"

"Because of them, I won't destroy the city," was the LORD's answer.

Finally, Abraham said, "Please don't get angry, LORD, if I speak just once more. Suppose you find only ten good people there."

"For the sake of ten good people," the LORD told him, "I still won't destroy the city."

After speaking with Abraham, the LORD left, and Abraham went back home.

## *Sodom and Gomorrah Destroyed*

Genesis
19.1-3a

That evening the two angels arrived in Sodom, while Lot was sitting near the city gate. When Lot saw them, he got up, bowed down low, and said, "Gentlemen, I am your servant. Please come to my home. You can wash your feet, spend the night, and be on your way in the morning."

They told him, "No, we'll spend the night in the city square." But Lot kept insisting, until they finally agreed and went home with him.

At night the two angels told Lot that God had sent them to destroy Sodom and that they were to lead him and his family to safety.

Genesis
19.15-28

Early the next morning the two angels tried to make Lot hurry and leave. They said, "Take your wife and your two daughters and get out of here as fast as you can! If you don't, every one of you will be killed when the LORD destroys the city." At first, Lot just stood there. But the LORD wanted to save him. So the angels took Lot, his wife, and his two daughters by the hand and led them out of the city. When they were outside, one of the angels said, "Run for your lives! Don't even look back. And don't stop in the valley. Run to the hills, where you will be safe."

Lot answered, "You have done us a great favor, sir. You have saved our lives, but please don't make us go to the hills. That's too far away. The city will be destroyed before we can get there, and we will be killed when it happens. There's a town near here. It's only a small place, but my family and I will be safe, if you let us go there."

"All right, go there," he answered. "I won't destroy that town. Hurry! Run! I can't do anything until you are safely there."

The town was later called Zoar because Lot had said it was small.

The sun was coming up as Lot reached the town of Zoar, and the LORD sent burning sulfur down like rain on Sodom and Gomorrah. He destroyed those cities and everyone who lived in them, as well as their land and the trees and grass that grew there.

On the way, Lot's wife looked back and was turned into a block of salt.

That same morning Abraham got up and went to the place where he had stood and spoken with the LORD. He looked down toward Sodom and Gomorrah and saw smoke rising from all over the land—it was like a flaming furnace.

## *Isaac Is Born*

Genesis
21.1-3,8

The LORD was good to Sarah and kept his promise. Although Abraham was very old, Sarah had a son exactly at the time God had said. Abraham named his son Isaac. . . .

The time came when Sarah no longer had to nurse Isaac, and on that day Abraham gave a big feast.

## Abraham Offers Isaac

Genesis
22.1-19

Some years later God decided to test Abraham, so he spoke to him.

Abraham answered, "Here I am, LORD."

The LORD said, "Go get Isaac, your only son, the one you dearly love! Take him to the land of Moriah, and I will show you a mountain where you must sacrifice him to me on the fires of an altar." So Abraham got up early the next morning and chopped wood for the fire. He put a saddle on his donkey and left with Isaac and two servants for the place where God had told him to go.

Three days later Abraham looked off in the distance and saw the place. He told his servants, "Stay here with the donkey, while my son and I go over there to worship. We will come back."

Abraham put the wood on Isaac's shoulder, but he carried the hot coals and the knife. As the two of them walked along, Isaac said, "Father, we have the coals and the wood, but where is the lamb for the sacrifice?"

"My son," Abraham answered, "God will provide the lamb."

The two of them walked on, and when they reached the place that God had told him about, Abraham built an altar and placed the wood on it. Next, he tied up his son and put him on the wood. He then took the knife and got ready to kill his son. But the LORD's angel shouted from heaven, "Abraham! Abraham!"

"Here I am!" he answered.

"Don't hurt the boy or harm him in any way!" the angel said. "Now I know that you truly obey God, because you were willing to offer him your only son."

Abraham looked up and saw a ram caught by its horns in the bushes. So he took the ram and sacrificed it in place of his son.

Abraham named that place "The LORD Will Provide." And even now people say, "On the mountain of the LORD it will be provided."

The LORD's angel called out from heaven a second time:

You were willing to offer the LORD your only son, and so he makes you this solemn promise, "I will bless you and give you such a large family, that someday your descendants will be more numerous than the stars in the sky or the grains of sand along the beach. They will defeat their enemies and take over the cities where their enemies live. You have obeyed me, and so you and your descendants will be a blessing to all nations on earth."

Abraham and Isaac went back to the servants who had come with him, and they returned to Abraham's home in Beersheba.

## Sarah and Abraham Die

Genesis
23.1,2a
When Sarah was one hundred twenty-seven years old, she died in Kiriath-Arba, better known as Hebron, in the land of Canaan.

After Sarah had died and Abraham was very old, Abraham said to the oldest servant in his house: "Go back to the country where I was born and find a wife for Isaac among my relatives." The servant left and came to the city where Nahor, Abraham's brother, lived. His son, Bethuel, had a beautiful daughter Rebekah and a son named Laban. It was God's will that Rebekah would become Isaac's wife. Her father and brother gave her permission to go with the servant. Her mother and brother gave her expensive gifts to take along. When Isaac saw Rebekah, he led her to his mother Sarah's tent and made her his wife. Isaac loved Rebekah and so overcame the loss of his mother.

Genesis
25.7,8,11
Abraham died at the ripe old age of one hundred seventy-five. . . .

God blessed Isaac after this, and Isaac moved to a place called "The Well of the Living One Who Sees Me."

# Jacob

## *Esau and Jacob*

Genesis
25.19-34

Isaac was the son of Abraham, and he was forty years old when he married Rebekah, the daughter of Bethuel. She was also the sister of Laban, the Aramean from northern Syria.

Almost twenty years later, Rebekah still had no children. So Isaac asked the LORD to let her have a child, and the LORD answered his prayer.

Before Rebekah gave birth, she knew she was going to have twins, because she could feel them inside her, fighting each other. She thought, "Why is this happening to me?" Finally, she asked the LORD why her twins were fighting, and he told her:

"Your two sons will become two separate nations.
The younger of the two will be stronger,
    and the older son will be his servant."

When Rebekah gave birth, the first baby was covered with red hair, so he was named Esau. The second baby grabbed on to his brother's heel, so they named him Jacob. Isaac was sixty years old when they were born.

As Jacob and Esau grew older, Esau liked the outdoors and became a good hunter, while Jacob settled down and became a shepherd. Esau would take the meat of wild animals to his father Isaac, and so Isaac loved him more, but Jacob was his mother's favorite son.

One day, Jacob was cooking some stew, when Esau came home hungry and said, "I'm starving to death! Give me some of that red stew right now!" That's how Esau got the name "Edom."

Jacob replied, "Sell me your rights as the first-born son."

"I'm about to die," Esau answered. "What good will those rights do me?"

But Jacob said, "Promise me your birthrights, here and now!"

31

And that's what Esau did. Jacob then gave Esau some bread and some of the bean stew, and when Esau had finished eating and drinking, he just got up and left, showing how little he thought of his rights as the first-born.

## Jacob Steals His Father's Blessing

Genesis
27.1-29
After Isaac had become old and almost blind, he called in his first-born son Esau, who asked him, "Father, what can I do for you?"

Isaac replied, "I am old and might die at any time. So take your bow and arrows, then go out in the fields, and kill a wild animal. Cook some of that tasty food that I love so much and bring it to me. I want to eat it once more and give you my blessing before I die."

Rebekah had been listening, and as soon as Esau left to go hunting, she said to Jacob, "I heard your father tell Esau to kill a wild animal and cook some tasty food for your father before he dies. Your father said this because he wants to bless your brother with the LORD as his witness. Now, my son, listen carefully to what I want you to do. Go and kill two of your best young goats and bring them to me. I'll cook the tasty food that your father loves so much. Then you can take it to him, so he can eat it and give you his blessing before he dies."

"My brother Esau is a hairy man," Jacob reminded her. "And I am not. If my father touches me and realizes I am trying to trick him, he will put a curse on me instead of giving me a blessing."

Rebekah insisted, "Let his curse fall on me! Just do what I say and bring me the meat." So Jacob brought the meat to his mother, and she cooked the tasty food that his father liked. Then she took Esau's best clothes and put them on Jacob. She also covered the smooth part of his hands and neck with goatskins and gave him some bread and the tasty food she had cooked.

Jacob went to his father and said, "Father, here I am."

"Which one of my sons are you?" his father asked.

Jacob replied, "I am Esau, your first-born, and I have done what you told me. Please sit up and eat the meat I have brought. Then you can give me your blessing."

Isaac asked, "My son, how did you find an animal so quickly?"

"The LORD your God was kind to me," Jacob answered.

"My son," Isaac said, "come closer, where I can touch you and find out if you really are Esau." Jacob went closer. His father touched him and said, "You sound like Jacob, but your hands feel hairy like Esau's." And so Isaac blessed Jacob, thinking he was Esau.

Isaac asked, "Are you really my son Esau?"

"Yes, I am," Jacob answered.

So Isaac told him, "Serve me the wild meat, and I can give you my blessing."

Jacob gave him some meat, and he ate it. He also gave him some wine, and he drank it. Then Isaac said, "Son, come over here and kiss me." While Jacob was kissing him, Isaac caught the smell of his clothes and said:

"The smell of my son
    is like a field the LORD has blessed.
God will bless you, my son, with dew from heaven
    and with fertile fields, rich with grain and grapes.
Nations will be your servants and bow down to you.
You will rule over your brothers,
    and they will kneel at your feet.
Anyone who curses you will be cursed;
    anyone who blesses you will be blessed."

## Esau Discovers He Has Been Deceived

Genesis
27.30-45

Right after Isaac had given Jacob his blessing and Jacob had gone, Esau came back from hunting. He cooked the tasty food, brought it to his father, and said, "Father, please sit up and eat the meat I have brought you, so you can give me your blessing."

"Who are you?" Isaac asked.

"I am Esau, your first-born son."

Isaac started trembling and said, "Then who brought me some wild meat right before you came in? I ate it and gave him a blessing that cannot be taken back."

Esau cried loudly and begged, "Father, give me a blessing too!"

Isaac answered, "Your brother tricked me and stole your blessing."

Esau replied, "My brother deserves the name Jacob, because he has already cheated me twice. The first time he cheated me out of my rights as the first-born son, and now he has cheated me out of my blessing." Then Esau asked his father, "Don't you still have any blessing left for me?"

"My son," Isaac answered, "I have made Jacob the ruler over you and your brothers, and all of you will be his servants. I have also promised him all the grain and grapes that he needs. There's nothing left that I can do for you."

"Father," Esau asked, "don't you have more than one blessing? You can surely give me a blessing too!" Then Esau started crying again.

So his father said:

"Your home will be far from that fertile land,
    where dew comes down from the heavens.
You will live by the power of your sword
    and be your brother's slave.
But when you decide to be free, you will break loose."

Esau hated his brother Jacob because he had stolen the blessing that was supposed to be his. So he said to himself, "Just as soon as my father dies, I'll kill Jacob."

When Rebekah found out what Esau planned to do, she sent for Jacob and told him, "Son, your brother Esau is just waiting for the time when he can kill you. Now listen carefully and do what I say.

Go to the home of my brother Laban in Haran and stay with him for a while. When Esau stops being angry and forgets what you have done to him, I'll send for you to come home. Why should I lose both of my sons on the same day?"

## Jacob's Dream

Genesis 28.10-21

Jacob left the town of Beersheba and started out for Haran. At sunset he stopped for the night and went to sleep, resting his head on a large rock. In a dream he saw a ladder that reached from earth to heaven, and God's angels were going up and down on it.

The LORD was standing beside the ladder and said:

I am the LORD God who was worshiped by Abraham and Isaac. I will give to you and your family the land on which you are now sleeping. Your descendants will spread over the earth in all directions and will become as numerous as the specks of dust. Your family will be a blessing to all people. Wherever you go, I will watch over you, then later I will bring you back to this land. I won't leave you—I will do all I have promised.

Jacob woke up suddenly and thought, "The LORD is in this place, and I didn't even know it." Then Jacob became frightened and said, "This is a fearsome place! It must be the house of God and the ladder to heaven."

When Jacob got up early the next morning, he took the rock that he had used for a pillow and stood it up for a place of worship. Then he poured olive oil on the rock to dedicate it to God, and he named the place Bethel. Before that it had been named Luz.

Jacob solemnly promised God, "If you go with me and watch over me as I travel, and if you give me food and clothes and bring me safely home again, you will be my God."

## Jacob with Laban

Jacob continued his journey and came to the country of Haran. There he settled down with his mother's brother Laban.

After Jacob had been there for a month, Laban said to him, "You shouldn't have to work without pay, just because you are a relative of mine. What do you want me to give you?"

Laban had two daughters. Leah was older than Rachel, but her eyes didn't sparkle, while Rachel was beautiful and had a good figure. Since Jacob was in love with Rachel, he answered, "If you will let me marry Rachel, I'll work seven years for you."

Laban replied, "It's better for me to let you marry Rachel than for someone else to have her. So stay and work for me." Jacob worked seven years for Laban, but the time seemed like only a few days, because he loved Rachel so much.

Jacob said to Laban, "The time is up, and I want to marry Rachel now!" So Laban gave a big feast and invited all their neighbors. But that evening he brought Leah to Jacob, who married her and spent the night with her. Laban also gave Zilpah to Leah as her servant woman.

The next morning Jacob found out that he had married Leah, and he asked Laban, "Why did you do this to me? Didn't I work to get Rachel? Why did you trick me?"

Laban replied, "In our country the older daughter must get married first. After you spend this week with Leah, you may also marry Rachel. But you will have to work for me another seven years."

At the end of the week of celebration, Laban let Jacob marry Rachel, and he gave her his servant woman Bilhah. Jacob loved Rachel more than he did Leah, but he had to work another seven years for Laban.

Jacob had eleven sons while he was serving Laban. Many times Laban had gone back on his word to reward Jacob. Nevertheless, Jacob became very rich.

## Jacob Wrestles

Jacob perceived that Laban and his sons were not as friendly to him as before. Then the LORD said to him: "Go back to your relatives in the land of your ancestors, and I will bless you." Jacob put his children and wives on camels, took his cattle and all the wealth he had accumulated and fled.

When they came to Jabbok River, he led them to the other side. Afterwards, Jacob went back and spent the night alone.

Genesis
32.24-32

A man came and fought with Jacob until just before daybreak. When the man saw that he could not win, he struck Jacob on the hip and threw it out of joint. They kept on wrestling until the man said, "Let go of me! It's almost daylight."

"You can't go until you bless me," Jacob replied.

Then the man asked, "What is your name?"

"Jacob," he answered.

The man said, "Your name will no longer be Jacob. You have wrestled with God and with men, and you have won. That's why your name will be Israel."

Jacob said, "Now tell me your name."

"Don't you know who I am?" he asked. And he blessed Jacob.

Jacob said, "I have seen God face to face, and I am still alive." So he named the place Peniel. The sun was coming up as Jacob was leaving Peniel. He was limping because he had been struck on the hip, and the muscle on his hip joint had been injured. That's why even today the people of Israel don't eat the hip muscle of any animal.

## Jacob Meets Esau

Jacob sent messengers ahead of him to his brother Esau, in the hope that his brother would be kind to him, and he prepared a big gift of goats, sheep, camels, cows, bulls, and donkeys. Jacob became very scared when his messengers came back and told him that Esau was coming with 400 men. So Jacob had his children walk with their mothers. The two servant women, Zilpah and Bilhah, together with their children went first, followed by Leah and her children, then by Rachel and Joseph. Jacob himself walked in front of them all, bowing to the ground seven times as he came near his brother.

Genesis
33.1b-11

But Esau ran toward Jacob and hugged and kissed him. Then the two brothers started crying.

When Esau noticed the women and children he asked, "Whose children are these?"

Jacob answered, "These are the ones the LORD has been kind enough to give to me, your servant."

Then the two servant women and their children came and bowed down to Esau. Next, Leah and her children came and bowed down; finally, Joseph and Rachel also came and bowed down.

Esau asked Jacob, "What did you mean by these herds I met along the road?"

"Master," Jacob answered, "I sent them so that you would be friendly to me."

"But, brother, I already have plenty," Esau replied. "Keep them for yourself."

"No!" Jacob said. "Please accept these gifts as a sign of your friendship for me. When you welcomed me and I saw your face, it was like seeing the face of God. Please accept these gifts I brought to you. God has been good to me, and I have everything I need." Jacob kept insisting until Esau accepted the gifts.

After this Jacob and Esau separated. Jacob and his family traveled ahead and settled in Canaan.

# Joseph and His Brothers

## *Joseph Shares His Dream*

Jacob—or Israel, as he also was called—lived in Canaan, where his father Isaac had lived as a foreigner. Jacob now had 12 sons: Reuben, Simeon, Levi, Judah, Issachar, Zebulun, Dan, Naphtali, Gad, Asher, Joseph, and Benjamin. The youngest were Rachel's sons.

Genesis
37.2b-11

When Jacob's son Joseph was seventeen years old, he took care of the sheep with his brothers, the sons of Bilhah and Zilpah. But he was always telling his father all sorts of bad things about his brothers.

Jacob loved Joseph more than he did any of his other sons, because Joseph was born after Jacob was very old. Jacob had given Joseph a fancy coat to show that he was his favorite son, and so Joseph's brothers hated him and would not be friendly to him.

One day, Joseph told his brothers what he had dreamed, and they hated him even more. Joseph said, "Let me tell you about my dream. We were out in the field, tying up bundles of wheat. Suddenly my bundle stood up, and your bundles gathered around and bowed down to it."

His brothers asked, "Do you really think you are going to be king and rule over us?" Now they hated Joseph more than ever because of what he had said about his dream.

Joseph later had another dream, and he told his brothers, "Listen to what else I dreamed. The sun, the moon, and eleven stars bowed down to me."

When he told his father about this dream, his father became angry and said, "What's that supposed to mean? Are your mother and I and your brothers all going to come and bow down in front of you?" Joseph's brothers were jealous of him, but his father kept wondering about the dream.

## The Brothers Sell Joseph

Genesis
37.12-14a

One day when Joseph's brothers had taken the sheep to a pasture near Shechem, his father Jacob said to him, "I want you to go to your brothers. They are with the sheep near Shechem."

"Yes, sir," Joseph answered.

His father said, "Go and find out how your brothers and the sheep are doing. Then come back and let me know."

Genesis
37.17b-35

Joseph left and found his brothers in Dothan. But before he got there, they saw him coming and made plans to kill him. They said to one another, "Look, here comes the hero of those dreams! Let's kill him and throw him into a pit and say that some wild animal ate him. Then we'll see what happens to those dreams."

Reuben heard this and tried to protect Joseph from them. "Let's not kill him," he said. "Don't murder him or even harm him. Just throw him into a dry well out here in the desert." Reuben planned to rescue Joseph later and take him back to his father.

When Joseph came to his brothers, they pulled off his fancy coat and threw him into a dry well.

As Joseph's brothers sat down to eat, they looked up and saw a caravan of Ishmaelites coming from Gilead. Their camels were loaded with all kinds of spices that they were taking to Egypt. So Judah said, "What will we gain if we kill our brother and hide his body? Let's sell him to the Ishmaelites and not harm him. After all, he is our brother." And the others agreed.

When the Midianite merchants came by, Joseph's brothers took him out of the well, and for twenty pieces of silver they sold him to the Ishmaelites who took him to Egypt.

When Reuben returned to the well and did not find Joseph there, he tore his clothes in sorrow. Then he went back to his brothers and said, "The boy is gone! What am I going to do?"

Joseph's brothers killed a goat and dipped Joseph's fancy coat in its blood. After this, they took the coat to their father and said, "We found this! Look at it carefully and see if it belongs to your son."

Jacob knew it was Joseph's coat and said, "It's my son's coat! Joseph has been torn to pieces and eaten by some wild animal."

Jacob mourned for Joseph a long time, and to show his sorrow he tore his clothes and wore sackcloth. All of Jacob's children came to comfort him, but he refused to be comforted. "No," he said, "I will go to my grave, mourning for my son." So Jacob kept on grieving.

## *Joseph Explains Some Prisoners' Dreams*

In Egypt Joseph was sold to Potiphar, one of Pharaoh's principal officials. Since the LORD helped Joseph to be successful in whatever he was doing, he gained Potiphar's favor and was put in charge of his palace.

But one day Potiphar's wife told her husband a lie about Joseph, and he had Joseph thrown into prison.

Genesis
40.1-23

While Joseph was in prison, both the king's personal servant and his chief cook made the king angry. So he had them thrown into the same prison with Joseph. They spent a long time in prison, and Potiphar, the official in charge of the palace guard, made Joseph their servant.

One night each of the two men had a dream, but their dreams had different meanings. The next morning, when Joseph went to see the men, he could tell they were upset, and he asked, "Why are you so worried today?"

"We each had a dream last night," they answered, "and there is no one to tell us what they mean."

Joseph replied, "Doesn't God know the meaning of dreams? Now tell me what you dreamed."

The king's personal servant told Joseph, "In my dream I saw a vine with three branches. As soon as it budded, it blossomed, and its grapes became ripe. I held the king's cup and squeezed the grapes into it, then I gave the cup to the king."

Joseph said:

This is the meaning of your dream. The three branches stand for three days, and in three days the king will pardon you. He will make you his personal servant again, and you will serve him his wine, just as you used to do. But when these good things happen, please don't forget to tell the king about me, so I can get out of this place. I was kidnapped from the land of the Hebrews, and here in Egypt I haven't done anything to deserve being thrown in jail.

When the chief cook saw that Joseph had given a good meaning to the dream, he told Joseph, "I also had a dream. In it I was carrying three breadbaskets stacked on top of my head. The top basket was full of all kinds of baked things for the king, but birds were eating them."

Joseph said:

This is the meaning of your dream. The three baskets are three days, and in three days the king will cut off your head. He will hang your body on a pole, and birds will come and peck at it.

Three days later, while the king was celebrating his birthday with a dinner for his officials, he sent for his personal servant and the chief cook. He put the personal servant back in his old job and had the cook put to death.

Everything happened just as Joseph had said it would, but the king's personal servant completely forgot about Joseph.

# Joseph Explains Pharaoh's Dreams

Genesis
41.1
Genesis
41.8-36

Two years later the king of Egypt dreamed he was standing beside the Nile River.

The next morning the king was upset. So he called in his magicians and wise men and told them what he had dreamed. None of them could tell him what the dreams meant.

The king's personal servant said:

Now I remember what I was supposed to do. When you were angry with me and your chief cook, you threw us both in jail in the house of the captain of the guard. One night we both had dreams, and each dream had a different meaning. A young Hebrew, who was a servant of the captain of the guard, was there with us at the time. When we told him our dreams, he explained what each of them meant, and everything happened just as he said it would. I got my job back, and the cook was put to death.

The king sent for Joseph, who was quickly brought out of jail. He shaved, changed his clothes, and went to the king.

The king said to him, "I had a dream, yet no one can explain what it means. I am told that you can interpret dreams."

"Your Majesty," Joseph answered, "I can't do it myself, but God can give a good meaning to your dreams."

The king told Joseph:

I dreamed I was standing on the bank of the Nile River. I saw seven fat, healthy cows come up out of the river, and they began feeding on the grass. Next, seven skinny, bony cows came up out of the river. I have never seen such terrible looking cows anywhere in Egypt. The skinny cows ate the fat ones. But you couldn't tell it, because these skinny cows were just as skinny as they were before. Right away, I woke up.

I also dreamed that I saw seven heads of grain growing on one stalk. The heads were full and ripe. Then seven other heads of grain came up. They were thin and scorched by a wind from the desert. These heads of grain swallowed the full ones. I told my dreams to the magicians, but none of them could tell me the meaning of the dreams.

Joseph replied:

Your Majesty, both of your dreams mean the same thing, and in them God has shown what he is going to do. The seven good cows stand for seven years, and so do the seven good heads of grain. The seven skinny, ugly cows that came up later also stand for seven years, as do the seven bad heads of grain that were scorched by the east wind. The dreams mean there will be seven years when there won't be enough grain.

It is just as I said—God has shown what he intends to do. For seven years Egypt will have more than enough grain, but that will be followed by seven years when there won't be enough. The good years of plenty will be forgotten, and everywhere in Egypt people will be starving. The famine will be so bad that no one will remember that once there had been plenty. God has given you two dreams to let you know that he has definitely decided to do this and that he will do it soon.

Your Majesty, you should find someone who is wise and will know what to do, so that you can put him in charge of all Egypt. Then appoint some other officials to collect one-fifth of every crop harvested in Egypt during the seven years when there is plenty. Give them the power to collect the grain during those good years and to store it in your cities. It can be stored until it is needed during the seven years when there won't be enough grain in Egypt. This will keep the country from being destroyed because of the lack of food.

Pharaoh found this plan good and said to Joseph: "Since God has given you all this knowledge, you are to be in charge of my palace and all people shall obey you. From now on you will rule over all of Egypt!"

In the seven years of plenty Joseph gathered all the grain and stored it. And when the seven years of famine started, he opened up the storehouses and sold grain to the Egyptians. People from all over the world came to Egypt to buy grain, for the famine was very severe all over the world.

## Joseph's Brothers Come to Egypt

Genesis
42.1-16

When Jacob found out there was grain in Egypt, he said to his sons, "Why are you just sitting here, staring at one another? I have heard there is grain in Egypt. Now go down and buy some, so we won't starve to death."

Ten of Joseph's brothers went to Egypt to buy grain. But Jacob did not send Joseph's younger brother Benjamin with them; he was afraid that something might happen to him. So Jacob's sons joined others from Canaan who were going to Egypt because of the terrible famine.

Since Joseph was governor of Egypt and in charge of selling grain, his brothers came to him and bowed with their faces to the ground. They did not recognize Joseph, but right away he knew who they were, though he pretended not to know. Instead, he spoke harshly and asked, "Where do you come from?"

"From the land of Canaan," they answered. "We've come here to buy grain."

Joseph remembered what he had dreamed about them and said, "You're spies! You've come here to find out where our country is weak."

"No sir," they replied. "We're your servants, and we have only come to buy grain. We're honest men, and we come from the same family—we're not spies."

"That isn't so!" Joseph insisted. "You've come here to find out where our country is weak."

But they explained, "Sir, we come from a family of twelve brothers. The youngest is still with our father in Canaan, and one of our brothers is dead."

Joseph replied:

It's just like I said. You're spies, and I'm going to find out who you really are. I swear by the life of the king that you won't leave this place until your youngest brother comes here. Choose one of you to go after your brother, while the rest of you stay here in jail. That will show whether you are telling the truth. But if you are lying, I swear by the life of the king that you are spies!

## Simeon Is Imprisoned

Genesis
42.17-38

Joseph kept his brothers all under guard for three days, before saying to them:

> Since I respect God, I'll give you a chance to save your lives. If you are honest men, one of you must stay here in jail, and the rest of you can take the grain back to your starving families. But you must bring your youngest brother to me. Then I'll know that you are telling the truth, and you won't be put to death.

Joseph's brothers agreed and said to one another, "We're being punished because of Joseph. We saw the trouble he was in, but we refused to help him when he begged us. That's why these terrible things are happening."

Reuben spoke up, "Didn't I tell you not to harm the boy? But you wouldn't listen, and now we have to pay the price for killing him."

They did not know that Joseph could understand them, since he was speaking through an interpreter. Joseph turned away from them and cried, but soon he turned back and spoke to them again. Then he had Simeon tied up and taken away while they watched.

Joseph gave orders for his brothers' grain sacks to be filled with grain and for their money to be put in their sacks. He also gave orders for them to be given food for their journey home. After this was done, they each loaded the grain on their donkeys and left.

When they stopped for the night, one of them opened his sack to get some grain for his donkey, and right away he saw his money-bag. "Here's my money!" he told his brothers. "Right here in my sack."

They were trembling with fear as they stared at one another and asked themselves, "What has God done to us?"

When they returned to the land of Canaan, they told their father Jacob everything that had happened to them:

> The governor of Egypt was rude and treated us like spies. But we told him, "We're honest men, not spies. We come from a family of twelve brothers. The youngest is still with our father in Canaan, and the other is dead."
>
> Then the governor of Egypt told us, "I'll find out if you really are honest. Leave one of your brothers here with me, while you

take the grain to your starving families. But bring your youngest brother to me, so I can be certain that you are honest men and not spies. After that, I'll let your other brother go free, and you can stay here and trade."

When the brothers started emptying their sacks of grain, they found their moneybags in them. They were frightened, and so was their father Jacob, who said, "You have already taken my sons Joseph and Simeon from me. And now you want to take away Benjamin! Everything is against me."

Reuben spoke up, "Father, if I don't bring Benjamin back, you can kill both of my sons. Trust me with him, and I will bring him back."

But Jacob said, "I won't let my son Benjamin go down to Egypt with the rest of you. His brother is already dead, and he is the only son I have left. I am an old man, and if anything happens to him on the way, I'll die from sorrow, and all of you will be to blame."

## Benjamin Comes to Egypt

Genesis
43.1-5

The famine in Canaan got worse, until finally, Jacob's family had eaten all the grain they had bought in Egypt. So Jacob said to his sons, "Go back and buy some more grain."

Judah replied, "The governor strictly warned us that we would not be allowed to see him unless we brought our youngest brother with us. If you let us take Benjamin along, we will go and buy grain. But we won't go without him!"

Genesis
43.11-34

Their father said:

If Benjamin must go with you, take the governor a gift of some of the best things from our own country, such as perfume, honey, spices, pistachio nuts, and almonds. Also take along twice the amount of money for the grain, because there must have been some mistake when the money was put back in your sacks. Take Benjamin with you and leave right away.

When you go in to see the governor, I pray that God All-Powerful will be good to you and that the governor will let your other brother and Benjamin come back home with you. If I must lose my children, I suppose I must.

The brothers took the gifts, twice the amount of money, and Benjamin. Then they hurried off to Egypt. When they stood in front of Joseph, he saw Benjamin and told the servant in charge of his house, "Take these men to my house. Slaughter an animal and cook it, so they can eat with me at noon."

The servant did as he was told and took the brothers to Joseph's house. But on the way they got worried and started thinking, "We are being taken there because of the money that was put back in our sacks last time. He will arrest us, make us his slaves, and take our donkeys."

So when they arrived at Joseph's house, they said to the servant in charge, "Sir, we came to Egypt once before to buy grain. But when we stopped for the night, we each found in our grain sacks the exact amount we had paid. We have brought that money back, together with enough money to buy more grain. We don't know who put the money in our sacks."

"It's all right," the servant replied. "Don't worry. The God you and your father worship must have put the money there, because I received your payment in full." Then he brought Simeon out to them.

The servant took them into Joseph's house and gave them water to wash their feet. He also tended their donkeys. The brothers got their gifts ready to give to Joseph at noon, since they had heard they were going to eat there.

When Joseph came home, they gave him the gifts they had brought, and they bowed down to him. After Joseph had asked how they were, he said, "What about your elderly father? Is he still alive?"

They answered, "Your servant our father is still alive and well." And again they bowed down to Joseph.

When Joseph looked around and saw his brother Benjamin, he said, "This must be your youngest brother, the one you told me about. God bless you, my son."

Right away he rushed off to his room and cried because of his love for Benjamin. After washing his face and returning, he was able to control himself and said, "Serve the meal!"

Joseph was served at a table by himself, and his brothers were served at another. The Egyptians sat at yet another table, because Egyptians felt it was disgusting to eat with Hebrews. To the surprise of Joseph's brothers, they were seated in front of him according to their ages, from the oldest to the youngest. They were served food from Joseph's table, and Benjamin was given five times as much as each of the others. So Joseph's brothers drank with him and had a good time.

## Joseph's Silver Cup

Genesis
44.1-18

Later, Joseph told the servant in charge of his house, "Fill the men's grain sacks with as much as they can hold and put their money in the sacks. Also put my silver cup in the sack of the youngest brother." The servant did as he was told.

Early the next morning, the men were sent on their way with their donkeys. But they had not gone far from the city when Joseph told the servant, "Go after those men! When you catch them, say, 'My master has been good to you. So why have you stolen his silver cup? Not only does he drink from his cup, but he also uses it to learn about the future. You have done a terrible thing.'"

When the servant caught up with them, he said exactly what Joseph had told him to say. But they replied, "Sir, why do you say such things? We would never do anything like that! We even returned the money we found in our grain sacks when we got back to Canaan. So why would we want to steal any silver or gold from your master's house? If you find that one of us has the cup, then kill him, and the rest of us will become your slaves."

"Good!" the man replied, "I'll do what you have said. But only the one who has the cup will become my slave. The rest of you can go free."

Each of the brothers quickly put his sack on the ground and opened it. Joseph's servant started searching the sacks, beginning with the one that belonged to the oldest brother. When he came to

Benjamin's sack, he found the cup. This upset the brothers so much that they began tearing their clothes in sorrow. Then they loaded their donkeys and returned to the city.

When Judah and his brothers got there, Joseph was still at home. So they bowed down to Joseph, who asked them, "What have you done? Didn't you know I could find out?"

"Sir, what can we say?" Judah replied. "How can we prove we are innocent? God has shown that we are guilty. And now all of us are your slaves, especially the one who had the cup."

Joseph told them, "I would never punish all of you. Only the one who was caught with the cup will become my slave. The rest of you are free to go home to your father."

Judah went over to Joseph and said:

Sir, you have as much power as the king himself, and I am only your slave. Please don't get angry if I speak.

Genesis
44.33,34

Sir, I am your slave. Please let me stay here in place of Benjamin and let him return home with his brothers. How can I face my father if Benjamin isn't with me? I couldn't bear to see my father in such sorrow.

## Joseph Reveals Who He Is

Genesis
45.1-5

Since Joseph could no longer control his feelings in front of his servants, he sent them out of the room. When he was alone with his brothers, he told them, "I am Joseph." Then he cried so loudly that the Egyptians heard him and told about it in the king's palace.

Joseph asked his brothers if his father was still alive, but they were too frightened to answer. Joseph told them to come closer to him, and when they did, he said:

Yes, I am your brother Joseph, the one you sold into Egypt. Don't worry or blame yourselves for what you did. God is the one who sent me ahead of you to save lives.

Genesis
45.9-15

Now hurry back and tell my father that his son Joseph says, "God has made me ruler of Egypt. Come here as quickly as you can. You will live near me in the region of Goshen with your children and grandchildren, as well as with your sheep, goats, cattle, and everything else you own. I will take care of you there during the next five years of famine. But if you don't come, you and your family and your animals will starve to death."

All of you, including my brother Benjamin, can tell by what I have said that I really am Joseph. Tell my father about my great power here in Egypt and about everything you have seen. Hurry and bring him here.

Joseph and Benjamin hugged each other and started crying. Joseph was still crying as he kissed each of his other brothers. After this, they started talking with Joseph.

## Jacob Travels to Egypt

Genesis
45.25-28

Joseph's brothers left Egypt, and when they arrived in Canaan, they told their father that Joseph was still alive and was the ruler of Egypt. But their father was so surprised that he could not believe them. Then they told him everything Joseph had said. When he saw the wagons Joseph had sent, he felt much better and said, "Now I can believe you! My son Joseph must really be alive, and I will get to see him before I die."

Jacob moved to Egypt with all that he owned and with his sons, grandsons, daughters and granddaughters, and with all of his relatives, sixty-six in all, not including his sons' wives.

Genesis
46.28-30

Jacob had sent his son Judah ahead of him to ask Joseph to meet them in Goshen. So Joseph got in his chariot and went to meet his father. When they met, Joseph hugged his father around the neck and cried for a long time. Jacob said to Joseph, "Now that I have seen you and know you are still alive, I am ready to die."

Jacob and his family settled in Goshen and they multiplied and became many. Jacob lived 17 years in Egypt. When his life was nearing the end, he called Joseph and said to him: "I won't live much longer. But God will be with you and will lead you back to the land he promised our family long ago."

Jacob commanded his sons to bury him in the cave at Machpelah at Mamre in Canaan. Abraham and his wife Sarah were buried there, as well as Isaac and his wife Rebekah and Jacob's wife Leah. After having given this instruction, Jacob died at 147 years of age.

## *Joseph Forgives His Brothers*

Genesis
50.15-22

After Jacob died, Joseph's brothers said to each other, "What if Joseph still hates us and wants to get even with us for all the cruel things we did to him?"

So they sent this message to Joseph:

Before our father died, he told us, "You did some cruel and terrible things to Joseph, but you must ask him to forgive you."

Now we ask you to please forgive the terrible things we did.

After all, we serve the same God that your father worshiped.

When Joseph heard this, he started crying.

Right then, Joseph's brothers came and bowed down to the ground in front of him and said, "We are your slaves."

But Joseph told them, "Don't be afraid! I have no right to change what God has decided. You tried to harm me, but God made it turn out for the best, so that he could save all these people, as he is now doing. Don't be afraid! I will take care of you and your children." After Joseph said this, his brothers felt much better.

Joseph lived in Egypt with his brothers until he died at the age of one hundred ten.

Before Joseph died, he told his brothers, "I won't live much longer. But God will take care of you and lead you out of Egypt to the land he promised Abraham, Isaac, and Jacob. Now promise me that you will take my body with you when God leads you to that land."

So Joseph died in Egypt at the age of one hundred ten; his body was embalmed and put in a coffin.

# The Israelites in Egypt

## The Israelites Are Mistreated in Egypt

Exodus
1.6-22

After Joseph, his brothers, and everyone else in that generation had died, the people of Israel became so numerous that the whole region of Goshen was full of them.

Many years later a new king came to power. He did not know what Joseph had done for Egypt, and he told the Egyptians:

There are too many of those Israelites in our country, and they are becoming more powerful than we are. If we don't outsmart them, their families will keep growing larger. And if our country goes to war, they could easily fight on the side of our enemies and escape from Egypt.

The Egyptians put slave bosses in charge of the people of Israel and tried to wear them down with hard work. Those bosses forced them to build the cities of Pithom and Rameses, where the king could store his supplies. But even though the Israelites were mistreated, their families grew larger, and they took over more land. Because of this, the Egyptians hated them worse than before and made them work so hard that their lives were miserable. The Egyptians were cruel to the people of Israel and forced them to make bricks and to mix mortar and to work in the fields.

Finally, the king called in Shiphrah and Puah, the two women who helped the Hebrew mothers when they gave birth. He told them, "If a Hebrew woman gives birth to a girl, let the child live. If the baby is a boy, kill him!"

But the two women were faithful to God and did not kill the boys, even though the king had told them to. The king called them in again and asked, "Why are you letting those baby boys live?"

They answered, "Hebrew women have their babies much quicker than Egyptian women. By the time we arrive, their babies are already born." God was good to the two women because they truly respected him, and he blessed them with children of their own.

The Hebrews kept increasing until finally, the king gave a command to everyone in the nation, "As soon as a Hebrew boy is born, throw him into the Nile River! But you can let the girls live."

## The Birth of Moses

Exodus
2.1-10

A man from the Levi tribe married a woman from the same tribe, and she later had a baby boy. He was a beautiful child, and she kept him inside for three months. But when she could no longer keep him hidden, she made a basket out of reeds and covered it with tar. She put him in the basket and placed it in the tall grass along the edge of the Nile River. The baby's older sister stood off at a distance to see what would happen to him.

About that time one of the king's daughters came down to take a bath in the river, while her servant women walked along the river bank. She saw the basket in the tall grass and sent one of the young women to pull it out of the water. When the king's daughter opened the basket, she saw the baby and felt sorry for him because he was crying. She said, "This must be one of the Hebrew babies."

At once the baby's older sister came up and asked, "Do you want me to get a Hebrew woman to take care of the baby for you?"

"Yes," the king's daughter answered.

So the girl brought the baby's mother, and the king's daughter told her, "Take care of this child, and I will pay you."

The baby's mother carried him home and took care of him. And when he was old enough, she took him to the king's daughter, who adopted him. She named him Moses because she said, "I pulled him out of the water."

60

## Moses Escapes

Exodus
2.11-15a

After Moses had grown up, he went out to where his own people were hard at work, and he saw an Egyptian beating one of them. Moses looked around to see if anyone was watching, then he killed the Egyptian and hid his body in the sand.

When Moses went out the next day, he saw two Hebrews fighting. So he went to the man who had started the fight and asked, "Why are you beating up one of your own people?"

The man answered, "Who put you in charge of us and made you our judge? Are you planning to kill me, just as you killed that Egyptian?"

This frightened Moses because he was sure that people must have found out what had happened. When the king heard what Moses had done, the king wanted to kill him. But Moses escaped and went to the land of Midian.

There Moses married Zipporah, who was the daughter of Jethro, the priest.

## God Calls Moses

Exodus
3.1-15

One day, Moses was taking care of the sheep and goats of his father-in-law Jethro, the priest of Midian, and Moses decided to lead them across the desert to Sinai, the holy mountain. There an angel of the LORD appeared to him from a burning bush. Moses saw that the bush was on fire, but it was not burning up. "This is strange!" he said to himself. "I'll go over and see why the bush isn't burning up."

When the LORD saw Moses coming near the bush, he called him by name, and Moses answered, "Here I am."

God replied, "Don't come any closer. Take off your sandals— the ground where you are standing is holy. I am the God who was worshiped by your ancestors Abraham, Isaac, and Jacob."

Moses was afraid to look at God, and so he hid his face.

The LORD said:

I have seen how my people are suffering as slaves in Egypt, and I have heard them beg for my help because of the way they are being mistreated. I feel sorry for them, and I have come down to rescue them from the Egyptians.

61

I will bring my people out of Egypt into a country where there is good land, rich with milk and honey. I will give them the land where the Canaanites, Hittites, Amorites, Perizzites, Hivites, and Jebusites now live. My people have begged for my help, and I have seen how cruel the Egyptians are to them. Now go to the king! I am sending you to lead my people out of his country.

But Moses said, "Who am I to go to the king and lead your people out of Egypt?"

God replied, "I will be with you. And you will know that I am the one who sent you, when you worship me on this mountain after you have led my people out of Egypt."

Moses answered, "I will tell the people of Israel that the God their ancestors worshiped has sent me to them. But what should I say, if they ask me your name?"

God said to Moses:

I am the eternal God. So tell them that the LORD, whose name is "I Am," has sent you. This is my name forever, and it is the name that people must use from now on.

God continued and said to Moses:

Exodus
3.19,20

But I know that the king of Egypt won't let you go unless something forces him to. So I will use my mighty power to perform all kinds of miracles and strike down the Egyptians. Then the king will send you away.

Moses returned to his father-in-law Jethro and asked for his permission to return to Egypt. He was granted permission, and he took his wife and his sons and left for Egypt.

Exodus
4.27-31

The LORD sent Aaron to meet Moses in the desert. So Aaron met Moses at Mount Sinai and greeted him with a kiss. Moses told Aaron what God had sent him to say; he also told him about the miracles God had given him the power to perform.

Later they brought together the leaders of Israel, and Aaron told them what the LORD had sent Moses to say. Then Moses worked the miracles for the people, and everyone believed. They bowed down and worshiped the LORD because they knew that he had seen their suffering and was going to help them.

## Pharaoh Refuses To Let the Israelites Leave the Country

Exodus
5.1,2

Moses and Aaron went to the king of Egypt and told him, "The LORD God says, 'Let my people go into the desert, so they can honor me with a celebration there.' "

"Who is this LORD and why should I obey him?" the king replied. "I refuse to let you and your people go!"

Exodus
5.6-9

That same day the king gave orders to his slave bosses and to the men directly in charge of the Israelite slaves. He told them:

Don't give the slaves any more straw to put in their bricks. Force them to find their own straw wherever they can, but they must make the same number of bricks as before. They are lazy, or else they would not beg me to let them go and sacrifice to their God. Make them work so hard that they won't have time to listen to these lies.

Exodus
5.22,23

Moses left them and prayed, "Our LORD, why have you brought so much trouble on your people? Is that why you sent me here? Ever since you told me to speak to the king, he has caused nothing but trouble for these people. And you haven't done a thing to help."

Exodus
6.1

The LORD God told Moses:

Soon you will see what I will do to the king. Because of my mighty power, he will let my people go, and he will even chase them out of his country.

## Aaron's Walking Stick Turns into a Snake

Exodus
7.8-13

The LORD said, "Moses, when the king asks you and Aaron to perform a miracle, command Aaron to throw his walking stick down in front of the king, and it will turn into a snake."

Moses and Aaron went to the king and his officials and did exactly as the LORD had commanded—Aaron threw the stick down, and it turned into a snake. Then the king called in the wise men and the magicians, who used their secret powers to do the same thing—they threw down sticks that turned into snakes. But Aaron's snake swallowed theirs. The king behaved just as the LORD had said and stubbornly refused to listen.

## The Ten Plagues

The LORD sent Moses and Aaron again and again to Pharaoh to tell about the terrible disasters that would fall on Egypt if Pharaoh would not let the Israelites leave the country.

Each plague was more terrible than the one before, but none of them touched Goshen where the Israelites lived. First, the water in the Nile turned to blood; then God sent frogs, followed by gnats and flies. Next a terrible disease caused the animals to die. Then the Egyptian people were infected with sores. Hailstones with thunder and lightning followed. Massive swarms of locusts covered the land and ate up everything that was growing. Finally, complete darkness fell over all of Egypt for three days so no one could see or leave their homes. But all of this made Pharaoh even more stubborn and he would not let the Israelites leave Egypt.

Exodus
11.1-10

The LORD said to Moses:

I am going to punish the king of Egypt and his people one more time. Then the king will gladly let you leave his land, so that I will stop punishing the Egyptians. He will even chase you out. Now go and tell my people to ask their Egyptian neighbors for gold and silver jewelry.

So the LORD made the Egyptians greatly respect the Israelites, and everyone, including the king and his officials, considered Moses an important leader.

Moses went to the king and said:

I have come to let you know what the LORD is going to do. About midnight he will go through the land of Egypt, and wherever he goes, the first-born son in every family will die. Your own son will die, and so will the son of the lowest slave woman. Even the first-born males of cattle will die. Everywhere in Egypt there will be loud crying. Nothing like this has ever happened before or will ever happen again.

But there won't be any need for the Israelites to cry. Things will be so quiet that not even a dog will be heard barking. Then you Egyptians will know that the LORD is good to the Israelites, even while he punishes you. Your leaders will come and bow down, begging me to take my people and leave your country. Then we will leave.

Moses was very angry; he turned and left the king.

What the LORD had earlier said to Moses came true. He had said, "The king of Egypt won't listen. Then I will perform even more miracles." So the king of Egypt saw Moses and Aaron work miracles, but the LORD made him stubbornly refuse to let the Israelites leave his country.

## The LORD Establishes the Passover

Exodus
12.1-13,17

Some time later the LORD said to Moses and Aaron:

This month is to be the first month of the year for you. Tell the people of Israel that on the tenth day of this month the head of each family must choose a lamb or a young goat for his family to eat. If any family is too small to eat the whole animal, they must share it with their next-door neighbors. Choose either a sheep or a goat, but it must be a one-year-old male that has nothing wrong with it. And it must be large enough for everyone to have some of the meat.

Each family must take care of its animal until the evening of the fourteenth day of the month, when the animals are to be killed. Some of the blood must be put on the two doorposts and above the door of each house where the animals are to be eaten. That night the animals are to be roasted and eaten, together with bitter herbs and thin bread made without yeast. Don't eat the meat raw or boiled. The entire animal, including its head, legs, and insides, must be roasted. Eat what you want that night, and the next morning burn whatever is left. When you eat the meal, be dressed and ready to travel. Have your sandals on, carry your walking stick in your hand, and eat quickly. This is the Passover Festival in honor of me, your LORD.

That same night I will pass through Egypt and kill the first-born son in every family and the first-born male of all animals. I am the LORD, and I will punish the gods of Egypt. The blood on the houses will show me where you live, and when I see the blood, I will pass over you. Then you won't be bothered by the terrible disasters I will bring on Egypt. . . .

Celebrate this Festival of Thin Bread as a way of remembering the day that I brought your families and tribes out of Egypt. And do this each year.

Moses called the leaders of Israel together and said:

Each family is to pick out a sheep and kill it for Passover. Make a brush from a few small branches of a hyssop plant and dip the brush in the bowl that has the blood of the animal in it. Then brush some of the blood above the door and on the posts at each side of the door of your house. After this, everyone is to stay inside.

During that night the LORD will go through the country of Egypt and kill the first-born son in every Egyptian family. He will see where you have put the blood, and he will not come into your house. His angel that brings death will pass over and not kill your first-born sons.

After you have entered the country promised to you by the LORD, you and your children must continue to celebrate Passover each year. Your children will ask you, "What are we celebrating?" And you will answer, "The Passover animal is killed to honor the LORD. We do these things because on that night long ago the LORD passed over the homes of our people in Egypt. He killed the first-born sons of the Egyptians, but he saved our children from death."

After Moses finished speaking, the people of Israel knelt down and worshiped the LORD. Then they left and did what Moses and Aaron had told them to do.

## The Israelites Leave Egypt

At midnight the LORD killed the first-born son of every Egyptian family, from the son of the king to the son of every prisoner in jail. He also killed the first-born male of every animal that belonged to the Egyptians.

That night the king, his officials, and everyone else in Egypt got up and started crying bitterly. In every Egyptian home, someone was dead.

During the night the king sent for Moses and Aaron and told them, "Get your people out of my country and leave us alone! Go and worship the LORD, as you have asked. Take your sheep, goats, and cattle, and get out. But ask your God to be kind to me."

The Egyptians did everything they could to get the Israelites to leave their country fast. They said, "Please hurry and leave. If you don't, we will all be dead." So the Israelites quickly made some bread dough and put it in pans. But they did not mix any yeast in the dough to make it rise. They wrapped cloth around the pans and carried them on their shoulders.

The Israelites had already done what Moses had told them to do. They had gone to their Egyptian neighbors and asked for gold and silver and for clothes. The LORD had made the Egyptians friendly toward the people of Israel, and they gave them whatever they asked for. In this way they carried away the wealth of the Egyptians when they left Egypt.

The Israelites walked from the city of Rameses to the city of Succoth. There were about six hundred thousand of them, not counting women and children. Many other people went with them as well, and there were also a lot of sheep, goats, and cattle. They left Egypt in such a hurry that they did not have time to prepare any food except the bread dough made without yeast. So they baked it and made thin bread.

The LORD's people left Egypt exactly four hundred thirty years after they had arrived.

# The LORD Rescues the Israelites

## *Leaving Egypt*

Exodus
13.17-22

After the king had finally let the people go, the LORD did not lead them through Philistine territory, though that was the shortest way. God had said, "If they are attacked, they may decide to return to Egypt." So he led them around through the desert and toward the Red Sea.

The Israelites left Egypt, prepared for battle.

Moses had them take along the bones of Joseph, whose dying words had been, "God will come to your rescue, and when he does, be sure to take along my bones."

The people of Israel left Succoth and camped at Etham at the border of Egypt near the desert. During the day the LORD went ahead of his people in a thick cloud, and during the night he went ahead of them in a flaming fire. That way the LORD could lead them at all times, whether day or night.

Exodus
14.5-14

When the king of Egypt heard that the Israelites had finally left, he and his officials changed their minds and said, "Look what we have done! We let them get away, and they will no longer be our slaves."

The king got his war chariot and army ready. He commanded his officers in charge of his six hundred best chariots and all his other chariots to start after the Israelites. The LORD made the king so stubborn that he went after them, even though the Israelites proudly went on their way. But the king's horses and chariots and soldiers caught up with them while they were camping by the Red Sea near Pi-Hahiroth and Baal-Zephon.

When the Israelites saw the king coming with his army, they were frightened and begged the LORD for help. They also complained to Moses, "Wasn't there enough room in Egypt to bury us? Is that why you brought us out here to die in the desert? Why did you bring us out of Egypt anyway? While we were there, didn't we tell you to leave us alone? We had rather be slaves in Egypt than die in this desert!"

But Moses answered, "Don't be afraid! Be brave, and you will see the LORD save you today. These Egyptians will never bother you again. The LORD will fight for you, and you won't have to do a thing."

## *The Israelites Cross the Sea*

Exodus
14.15-31

The LORD said to Moses, "Why do you keep calling out to me for help? Tell the Israelites to move forward. Then hold your walking stick over the sea. The water will open up and make a road where they can walk through on dry ground. I will make the Egyptians so stubborn that they will go after you. Then I will be praised because of what happens to the king and his chariots and cavalry. The Egyptians will know for sure that I am the LORD."

All this time God's angel had gone ahead of Israel's army, but now he moved behind them. A large cloud had also gone ahead of them, but now it moved between the Egyptians and the Israelites. The cloud gave light to the Israelites, but made it dark for the Egyptians, and during the night they could not come any closer.

Moses stretched his arm over the sea, and the LORD sent a strong east wind that blew all night until there was dry land where the water had been. The sea opened up, and the Israelites walked through on dry land with a wall of water on each side.

The Egyptian chariots and cavalry went after them. But before daylight the LORD looked down at the Egyptian army from the fiery cloud and made them panic. Their chariot wheels got stuck, and it was hard for them to move. So the Egyptians said to one another, "Let's leave these people alone! The LORD is on their side and is fighting against us."

The LORD told Moses, "Stretch your arm toward the sea—the water will cover the Egyptians and their cavalry and chariots." Moses stretched out his arm, and at daybreak the water rushed toward the Egyptians. They tried to run away, but the LORD drowned them in the sea. The water came and covered the chariots, the cavalry, and the whole Egyptian army that had followed the Israelites

into the sea. Not one of them was left alive. But the sea had made a wall of water on each side of the Israelites; so they walked through on dry land.

On that day, when the Israelites saw the bodies of the Egyptians washed up on the shore, they knew that the LORD had saved them. Because of the mighty power he had used against the Egyptians, the Israelites worshiped him and trusted him and his servant Moses.

## Miriam's Song of Praise to God

Exodus
15.20,21

Miriam the sister of Aaron was a prophet. So she took her tambourine and led the other women out to play their tambourines and to dance. Then she sang to them:

"Sing praises to the LORD for his great victory!
He has thrown the horses and their riders into the sea."

# The Israelites in the Desert

### *The LORD Sends the Israelites Food*

Moses led the people from the Red Sea into the desert of Shur. After a while they came to Elim where there were twelve springs and seventy palm trees; they settled down there.

Exodus
16.1-21

On the fifteenth day of the second month after the Israelites had escaped from Egypt, they left Elim and started through the western edge of the Sinai Desert in the direction of Mount Sinai. There in the desert they started complaining to Moses and Aaron, "We wish the LORD had killed us in Egypt. When we lived there, we could at least sit down and eat all the bread and meat we wanted. But you have brought us out here into this desert, where we are going to starve."

The LORD said to Moses, "I will send bread down from heaven like rain. Each day the people can go out and gather only enough for that day. That's how I will see if they obey me. But on the sixth day of each week they must gather and cook twice as much."

Moses and Aaron told the people, "This evening you will know that the LORD was the one who rescued you from Egypt. And in the morning you will see his glorious power, because he has heard your complaints against him. Why should you grumble to us? Who are we?"

Then Moses continued, "You will know it is the LORD when he gives you meat each evening and more than enough bread each morning. He is really the one you are complaining about, not us—we are nobodies—but the LORD has heard your complaints."

Moses turned to Aaron and said, "Bring the people together, because the LORD has heard their complaints."

Aaron was speaking to them, when everyone looked out toward the desert and saw the bright glory of the LORD in a cloud. The LORD said to Moses, "I have heard my people complain. Now tell

them that each evening they will have meat and each morning they will have more than enough bread. Then they will know that I am the LORD their God."

That evening a lot of quails came and landed everywhere in the camp, and the next morning dew covered the ground. After the dew had gone, the desert was covered with thin flakes that looked like frost. The people had never seen anything like this, and they started asking each other, "What is it?"

Moses answered, "This is the bread that the LORD has given you to eat. And he orders you to gather about two quarts for each person in your family—that should be more than enough."

They did as they were told. Some gathered more and some gathered less, according to their needs, and none was left over.

Moses told them not to keep any overnight. Some of them disobeyed, but the next morning what they kept was stinking and full of worms, and Moses was angry.

Each morning everyone gathered as much as they needed, and in the heat of the day the rest melted.

Exodus
16.31
The Israelites called the bread manna. It was white like coriander seed and delicious as wafers made with honey.

Exodus
16.35,36
The Israelites ate manna for forty years, before they came to the border of Canaan that was a settled land.

## Water Comes out from the Rock

Exodus
17.1-6
The Israelites left the desert and moved from one place to another each time the LORD ordered them to. Once they camped at Rephidim, but there was no water for them to drink.

The people started complaining to Moses, "Give us some water!"

Moses replied, "Why are you complaining to me and trying to put the LORD to the test?"

But the people were thirsty and kept on complaining, "Moses, did you bring us out of Egypt just to let us and our families and our animals die of thirst?"

Then Moses prayed to the LORD, "What am I going to do with these people? They are about to stone me to death!"

The LORD answered, "Take some of the leaders with you and go ahead of the rest of the people. Also take along the walking stick you used to strike the Nile River, and when you get to the rock at Mount Sinai, I will be there with you. Strike the rock with the stick, and water will pour out for the people to drink." Moses did this while the leaders watched.

Thus the LORD took care of the Israelites in the desert.

## *War with the Amalekites*

Exodus
17.8-13

When the Israelites were at Rephidim, they were attacked by the Amalekites. So Moses told Joshua, "Have some men ready to attack the Amalekites tomorrow. I will stand on a hilltop, holding this walking stick that has the power of God."

Joshua led the attack as Moses had commanded, while Moses, Aaron, and Hur stood on the hilltop. The Israelites out-fought the Amalekites as long as Moses held up his arms, but they started losing whenever he had to lower them. Finally, Moses was so tired that Aaron and Hur got a rock for him to sit on. Then they stood beside him and supported his arms in the same position until sunset. That's how Joshua defeated the Amalekites.

# The LORD Meets with His People

## *The Ten Commandments*

Exodus
19.1,2

Exodus
19.20

Exodus
20.1-17

The Israelites left Rephidim. Then two months after leaving Egypt, they arrived at the desert near Mount Sinai, where they set up camp at the foot of the mountain.

The LORD came down to the top of Mount Sinai and told Moses to meet him there.

God said to the people of Israel:

I am the LORD your God, the one who brought you out of Egypt where you were slaves.

Do not worship any god except me.

Do not make idols that look like anything in the sky or on earth or in the ocean under the earth. Don't bow down and worship idols. I am the LORD your God, and I demand all your love. If you reject me, I will punish your families for three or four generations. But if you love me and obey my laws, I will be kind to your families for thousands of generations.

Do not misuse my name. I am the LORD your God, and I will punish anyone who misuses my name.

Remember that the Sabbath Day belongs to me. You have six days when you can do your work, but the seventh day of each week belongs to me, your God. No one is to work on that day—not you, your children, your slaves, your animals, or the foreigners who live in your towns. In six days I made the sky, the earth, the oceans, and everything in them, but on the seventh day I rested. That's why I made the Sabbath a special day that belongs to me.

Respect your father and your mother, and you will live a long time in the land I am giving you.

Do not murder.

Be faithful in marriage.

Do not steal.

Do not tell lies about others.

Do not want anything that belongs to someone else. Don't want anyone's house, wife or husband, slaves, oxen, donkeys or anything else.

## The Sacred Chest

Exodus
24.12-14

The LORD said to Moses, "Come up on the mountain and stay here for a while. I will give you the two flat stones on which I have written the laws that my people must obey." Moses and Joshua his assistant got ready, then Moses started up the mountain to meet with God.

Moses had told the leaders, "Wait here until we come back. Aaron and Hur will be with you, and they can settle any arguments while we are away."

The LORD told Moses to build a chest of acacia wood and to cover it with gold, to make four carrying rings of gold for it and attach them to its four legs. Further the LORD told Moses to make carrying poles of acacia wood and cover them with gold and put them through the rings, so that the chest could be carried. The LORD then told Moses to put the Ten Commandments, written on the two flat stones, inside the chest.

Moses stayed on the mountain for 40 days and 40 nights.

## The Golden Calf

Exodus
32.1-8

After the people saw that Moses had been on the mountain for a long time, they went to Aaron and said, "Make us an image of a god who will lead and protect us. Moses brought us out of Egypt, but nobody knows what has happened to him."

Aaron told them, "Bring me the gold earrings that your wives and sons and daughters are wearing." Everybody took off their earrings and brought them to Aaron, then he melted them and made an idol in the shape of a young bull.

All the people said to one another, "This is the god who brought us out of Egypt!"

When Aaron saw what was happening, he built an altar in front of the idol and said, "Tomorrow we will celebrate in honor of the LORD." The people got up early the next morning and killed some animals to be used for sacrifices and others to be eaten. Then everyone ate and drank so much that they began to carry on like wild people.

The LORD said to Moses:

Hurry back down! Those people you led out of Egypt are acting like fools. They have already stopped obeying me and have made themselves an idol in the shape of a young bull. They have bowed down to it, offered sacrifices, and said that it is the god who brought them out of Egypt.

Moses went back down the mountain with the two flat stones on which God had written all of his laws with his own hand, and he had used both sides of the stones.

When Joshua heard the noisy shouts of the people, he said to Moses, "A battle must be going on down in the camp."

But Moses replied, "It doesn't sound like they are shouting because they have won or lost a battle. They are singing wildly!"

As Moses got closer to the camp, he saw the idol, and he also saw the people dancing around. This made him so angry that he threw down the stones and broke them to pieces at the foot of the mountain. He melted the idol the people had made, and he ground it into powder. He scattered it in their water and made them drink it.

Exodus
32.30-35

The next day Moses told the people, "This is a terrible thing you have done. But I will go back to the LORD to see if I can do something to keep this sin from being held against you."

Moses returned to the LORD and said, "The people have committed a terrible sin. They have made a gold idol to be their god. But I beg you to forgive them. If you don't, please wipe my name out of your book."

The LORD replied, "I will wipe out of my book the name of everyone who has sinned against me. Now take my people to the place I told you about, and my angel will lead you. But when the time comes, I will punish them for this sin."

So the LORD punished the people of Israel with a terrible disease for talking Aaron into making the gold idol.

## Moses Receives the New Stone Tablets

Exodus
34.1,2

One day the LORD said to Moses, "Cut two flat stones like the first ones I made, and I will write on them the same commandments that were on the two you broke. Be ready tomorrow morning to come up Mount Sinai and meet me at the top.

Exodus
34.4

So Moses cut two flat stones like the first ones, and early the next morning he carried them to the top of Mount Sinai, just as the LORD had commanded.

Exodus
34.28

Moses stayed on the mountain with the LORD for forty days and nights, without eating or drinking. And he wrote down the Ten Commandments, the most important part of God's agreement with his people.

The LORD told the Israelites to make a sacred tent where they could meet with him. He gave Moses detailed instructions concerning how it should look and what it should contain, such as the sacred chest, the stone tablets, the menorah, and the altar for burning incense. The LORD said that Aaron and his sons would be the priests in the holy place.

## The LORD's Blessing

Numbers
6.22-27

The LORD told Moses, "When Aaron and his sons bless the people of Israel, they must say:

I pray that the LORD will bless and protect you,
    and that he will show you mercy and kindness.
May the LORD be good to you and give you peace."

Then the LORD said, "If Aaron and his sons ask me to bless the Israelites, I will give them my blessing."

81

# On the Way to Canaan

## The Israelites Explore the Land

The LORD said to Moses, "Choose a leader from each tribe and send them into Canaan to explore the land I am giving you."

Before Moses sent them into Canaan, he said:

After you go through the Southern Desert of Canaan, continue north into the hill country and find out what those regions are like. Be sure to remember how many people live there, how strong they are, and if they live in open towns or walled cities. See if the land is good for growing crops and find out what kinds of trees grow there. It's time for grapes to ripen, so try to bring back some of the fruit that grows there.

The twelve men left to explore Canaan from the Zin Desert in the south all the way to the town of Rehob near Lebo-Hamath in the north. . . .

When they got to Bunch Valley, they cut off a branch with such a huge bunch of grapes, that it took two men to carry it on a pole. That's why the place was called Bunch Valley. Along with the grapes, they also took back pomegranates and figs.

After exploring the land of Canaan forty days, the twelve men returned to Kadesh in the Paran Desert and told Moses, Aaron, and the people what they had seen. They showed them the fruit and said:

Look at this fruit! The land we explored is rich with milk and honey. But the people who live there are strong, and their cities are large and walled. We even saw the three Anakim clans. Besides that, the Amalekites live in the Southern Desert; the Hittites, Jebusites, and Amorites are in the hill country; and the Canaanites live along the Mediterranean Sea and the Jordan River.

## The Israelites Complain

Numbers
14.1-4

After the Israelites heard the report from the twelve men who had explored Canaan, the people cried all night and complained to Moses and Aaron, "We wish we had died in Egypt or somewhere out here in the desert! Is the LORD leading us into Canaan, just to have us killed and our women and children captured? We'd be better off in Egypt." Then they said to one another, "Let's choose our own leader and go back."

The LORD became very angry with the Israelites because they revolted against him. They had to wander in the desert for forty years as punishment for having opposed the LORD.

## The Snake Made of Bronze

The Israelites reached Mount Hor at the border of Edom where Aaron died.

Numbers
21.4-9

The Israelites had to go around the territory of Edom, so when they left Mount Hor, they headed south toward the Red Sea. But along the way, the people became so impatient that they complained against God and said to Moses, "Did you bring us out of Egypt, just to let us die in the desert? There's no water out here, and we can't stand this awful food!"

Then the LORD sent poisonous snakes that bit and killed many of them.

Some of the people went to Moses and admitted, "It was wrong of us to insult you and the LORD. Now please ask him to make these snakes go away."

Moses prayed, and the LORD answered, "Make a snake out of bronze and place it on top of a pole. Anyone who gets bitten can look at the snake and won't die."

Moses obeyed the LORD. And all of those who looked at the bronze snake lived, even though they had been bitten by the poisonous snakes.

84

## Moses Speaks to the People

When the 40 years of wandering were over, the Israelites were in the desert east of the Jordan River. It was there that Moses told the people of Israel the words of God:

Deuteronomy 6.4-13

Listen, Israel! The LORD our God is the only true God! So love the LORD your God with all your heart, soul, and strength. Memorize his laws and tell them to your children over and over again. Talk about them all the time, whether you're at home or walking along the road or going to bed at night, or getting up in the morning. Write down copies and tie them to your wrists and foreheads to help you obey them. Write these laws on the door frames of your homes and on your town gates.

The LORD promised your ancestors Abraham, Isaac, and Jacob that he would give you this land. Now he will take you there and give you large towns, with good buildings that you didn't build, and houses full of good things that you didn't put there. The LORD will give you wells that you didn't have to dig, and vineyards and olive orchards that you didn't have to plant. But when you have eaten so much that you can't eat any more, don't forget it was the LORD who set you free from slavery and brought you out of Egypt. Worship and obey the LORD your God with fear and trembling, and promise that you will be loyal to him.

When Moses had finished speaking, he climbed Mount Nebo. There the LORD showed him the whole country and told him: "This is the land I was talking about when I solemnly promised Abraham, Isaac, and Jacob that I would give land to their descendants." Moses died when he was 120 years old.

# The Promised Land

## *Joshua Becomes Israel's Leader*

After Moses had died, the LORD said to Joshua, the son of Nun:

Joshua

1.2-11

My servant Moses is dead. Now you must lead Israel across the Jordan River into the land I'm giving to all of you. Wherever you go, I'll give you that land, as I promised Moses. It will reach from the Southern Desert to the Lebanon Mountains in the north, and to the northeast as far as the great Euphrates River. It will include the land of the Hittites, and the land from here at the Jordan River to the Mediterranean Sea on the west. Joshua, I will always be with you and help you as I helped Moses, and no one will ever be able to defeat you.

Long ago I promised the ancestors of Israel that I would give this land to their descendants. So be strong and brave! Be careful to do everything my servant Moses taught you. Never stop reading *The Book of the Law* he gave you. Day and night you must think about what it says. If you obey it completely, you and Israel will be able to take this land.

I've commanded you to be strong and brave. Don't ever be afraid or discouraged! I am the LORD your God, and I will be there to help you wherever you go.

Joshua ordered the tribal leaders to go through the camp and tell everyone:

In a few days we will cross the Jordan River to take the land that the LORD our God is giving us. So fix as much food as you'll need for the march into the land.

Joshua sent two men to spy on the land. In Jericho they would have been taken captive, but a woman named Rahab helped them to escape.

## The Israelites Cross over Jordan

Joshua
3.1

Early the next morning, Joshua and the Israelites packed up and left Acacia. They went to the Jordan River and camped there that night.

Joshua
3.5-8

Joshua told the people, "Make yourselves acceptable to worship the LORD, because he is going to do some amazing things for us."

Then Joshua turned to the priests and said, "Take the chest and cross the Jordan River ahead of us." So the priests picked up the chest by its carrying poles and went on ahead.

The LORD told Joshua, "Beginning today I will show the people that you are their leader, and they will know that I am helping you as I helped Moses. Now, tell the priests who are carrying the chest to go a little way into the river and stand there."

Joshua
3.14-17

The Israelites packed up and left camp. The priests carrying the chest walked in front, until they came to the Jordan River. The water in the river had risen over its banks, as it often does in springtime. But as soon as the feet of the priests touched the water, the river stopped flowing, and the water started piling up at the town of Adam near Zarethan. No water flowed toward the Dead Sea, and the priests stood in the middle of the dry riverbed near Jericho while everyone else crossed over.

Joshua
4.14-19

"Joshua," the LORD said, "have the priests come up from the Jordan and bring the chest with them." So Joshua went over to the priests and told them what the LORD had said. And as soon as the priests carried the chest past the highest place that the floodwaters of the Jordan had reached, the river flooded its banks again.

That's how the LORD showed the Israelites that Joshua was their leader. For the rest of Joshua's life, they respected him as they had respected Moses.

It was the tenth day of the first month of the year when Israel crossed the Jordan River. They set up camp at Gilgal, which was east of the land controlled by Jericho.

## The Walls of Jericho Fall Down

Joshua
6.1-25

Meanwhile, the people of Jericho had been locking the gates in their town wall because they were afraid of the Israelites. No one could go out or come in.

The LORD said to Joshua:

With my help, you and your army will defeat the king of Jericho and his army, and you will capture the town. Here is how to do it: March slowly around Jericho once a day for six days. Take along the sacred chest and have seven priests walk in front of it, carrying trumpets.

But on the seventh day, march slowly around the town seven times while the priests blow their trumpets. Then the priests will blast on their trumpets, and everyone else will shout. The wall will fall down, and your soldiers can go straight in from every side.

Joshua called the priests together and said, "Take the chest and have seven priests carry trumpets and march ahead of it."

Next, he gave the army their orders: "March slowly around Jericho. A few of you will go ahead of the chest to guard it, but most of you will follow it. Don't shout the battle cry or yell or even talk until the day I tell you to. Then let out a shout!"

As soon as Joshua finished giving the orders, the army started marching. One group of soldiers led the way, with seven priests marching behind them and blowing trumpets. Then came the priests carrying the chest, followed by the rest of the soldiers. They obeyed Joshua's orders and carried the chest once around the town before returning to camp for the night.

Early the next morning, Joshua and everyone else started marching around Jericho in the same order as the day before. One group of soldiers was in front, followed by the seven priests with trumpets and the priests who carried the chest. The rest of the army came next. The seven priests blew their trumpets while everyone marched slowly around Jericho and back to camp. They did this once a day for six days.

On the seventh day, the army got up at daybreak. They marched slowly around Jericho the same as they had done for the past six days, except on this day they went around seven times.

Then the priests blew the trumpets, and Joshua yelled:

Get ready to shout! The LORD will let you capture this town. But you must destroy it and everything in it, to show that it now belongs to the LORD. The woman Rahab helped the spies we sent, so protect her and the others who are inside her house. But kill everyone else in the town. The silver and gold and everything made of bronze and iron belong to the LORD and must be put in his treasury. Be careful to follow these instructions, because if you see something you want and take it, the LORD will destroy Israel. And it will be all your fault.

The priests blew their trumpets again, and the soldiers shouted as loud as they could. The walls of Jericho fell flat. Then the soldiers rushed up the hill, went straight into the town, and captured it. They killed everyone, men and women, young and old, everyone except Rahab and the others in her house. They even killed every cow, sheep, and donkey.

Joshua said to the two men who had been spies, "Rahab kept you safe when I sent you to Jericho. We promised to protect her and her family, and we will keep that promise. Now go into her house and bring them out."

The two men went into Rahab's house and brought her out, along with her father and mother, her brothers, and her other relatives. Rahab and her family had to stay in a place just outside the Israelite army camp. But later they were allowed to live among the Israelites, and her descendants still do.

The Israelites took the silver and gold and the things made of bronze and iron and put them with the rest of the treasure that was kept at the LORD's house. Finally, they set fire to Jericho and everything in it.

After this Joshua captured the entire land. Every tribe received certain territory and settled there. The LORD let the Israelites defeat all of their enemies and he granted them peace. Thus the promises given by the LORD to the Israelites' ancestors were fulfilled.

## Joshua Speaks to the People

Joshua
24.14b-18

After a long time, when Joshua had grown old, he called the nation of Israel together and spoke to them:

Worship the LORD, obey him, and always be faithful. Get rid of the idols your ancestors worshiped when they lived on the other side of the Euphrates River and in Egypt. But if you don't want to worship the LORD, then choose right now! Will you worship the same idols your ancestors did? Or since you're living on land that once belonged to the Amorites, maybe you'll worship their gods. I won't. My family and I are going to worship and obey the LORD!

The people answered:

We could never worship other gods or stop worshiping the LORD. The LORD is our God. We were slaves in Egypt as our ancestors had been, but we saw the LORD work miracles to set our people free and to bring us out of Egypt. Even though other nations were all around us, the LORD protected us wherever we went. And when we fought the Amorites and the other nations that lived in this land, the LORD made them run away. Yes, we will worship and obey the LORD, because the LORD is our God.

## The Israelites Stop Worshiping the LORD

Judges
2.6-15

Joshua had been faithful to the LORD. And after Joshua sent the Israelites to take the land they had been promised, they remained faithful to the LORD until Joshua died at the age of one hundred ten. He was buried on his land in Timnath-Heres, in the hill country of Ephraim north of Mount Gaash. Even though Joshua was gone, the Israelites were faithful to the LORD during the lifetime of those men who had been leaders with Joshua and who had seen the wonderful things the LORD had done for Israel.

After a while the people of Joshua's generation died, and the next generation did not know the LORD or any of the things he had done for Israel. The LORD had brought their ancestors out of Egypt, and they had worshiped him. But now the Israelites stopped worshiping the LORD and worshiped the idols of Baal and Astarte, as well as the idols of other gods from nearby nations.

The LORD was so angry at the Israelites that he let other nations raid Israel and steal their crops and other possessions. Enemies were everywhere, and the LORD always let them defeat Israel in battle. The LORD had warned Israel he would do this, and now the Israelites were miserable.

This was a bad time for Israel. People did not obey the LORD but turned to other gods, and the LORD let the enemies attack the land. But when they asked God for help, he gave them leaders who freed them from the hands of their enemies. These leaders were called judges. They were sent by God to help the Israelites and to show them what was right.

## Deborah

Later on, Jabin, a Canaanite king, conquered the Israelites. He ruled the Israelites and oppressed them for 20 years.

Judges
4.4-10

Deborah the wife of Lappidoth was a prophet and a leader of Israel during those days. She would sit under Deborah's Palm Tree between Ramah and Bethel in the hill country of Ephraim, where Israelites would come and ask her to settle their legal cases.

One day, Barak the son of Abinoam was in Kedesh in Naphtali, and Deborah sent word for him to come and talk with her. When he arrived, she said:

I have a message for you from the LORD God of Israel! You are to get together an army of ten thousand men from the Naphtali and Zebulun tribes and lead them to Mount Tabor. The LORD will trick Sisera into coming out to fight you at the Kishon River. Sisera will be leading King Jabin's army as usual, and they will have their chariots, but the LORD has promised to help you defeat them.

"I'm not going unless you go!" Barak told her.

"All right, I'll go!" she replied. "But I'm warning you that the LORD is going to let a woman defeat Sisera, and no one will honor you for winning the battle."

Deborah and Barak left for Kedesh, where Barak called together the troops from Zebulun and Naphtali. Ten thousand soldiers gathered there, and Barak led them out from Kedesh. Deborah went too.

Judges
4.12-16

When Sisera learned that Barak had led an army to Mount Tabor, he called his troops together and got all nine hundred iron chariots ready. Then he led his army away from Harosheth-Ha-Goiim to the Kishon River.

Deborah shouted, "Barak, it's time to attack Sisera! Because today the LORD is going to help you defeat him. In fact, the LORD has already gone on ahead to fight for you."

Barak led his ten thousand troops down from Mount Tabor. And during the battle, the LORD confused Sisera, his chariot drivers, and his whole army. Everyone was so afraid of Barak and his army, that even Sisera jumped down from his chariot and tried to escape. Barak's forces went after Sisera's chariots and army as far as Harosheth-Ha-Goiim.

Sisera's entire army was wiped out.

Judges
4.24

Jabin grew weaker while the Israelites kept growing stronger, and at last the Israelites destroyed him.

## The Birth of Samson

Judges
13.1-5

Once again the Israelites started disobeying the LORD. So he let the Philistines take control of Israel for forty years.

Manoah from the tribe of Dan lived in the town of Zorah. His wife was not able to have children, but one day an angel from the LORD appeared to her and said:

> You have never been able to have any children, but very soon you will be pregnant and have a son. He will belong to God from the day he is born, so his hair must never be cut. And even before he is born, you must not drink any wine or beer or eat any food forbidden by God's laws.
>
> Your son will begin to set Israel free from the Philistines.

Judges
13.24,25

Later, Manoah's wife did give birth to a son, and she named him Samson. As the boy grew, the LORD blessed him. Then, while Samson was staying at Dan's Camp between the towns of Zorah and Eshtaol, the Spirit of the LORD took control of him.

## Samson Burns the Philistine Wheatfields

When Samson was grown up, he fell in love with a Philistine woman and wanted to marry her. At first, his father and mother were against it for they did not know that through this the LORD would bring trouble to the Philistines who ruled over Israel. Samson's parents eventually agreed and Samson married her. But during the wedding celebration, Samson was tricked by thirty young Philistines, so he got mad and returned to his home and family.

Later, during the wheat harvest, Samson went to visit the young woman he thought was still his wife. He brought along a young goat as a gift and said to her father, "I want to go into my wife's bedroom."

"You can't do that," he replied. "When you left the way you did, I thought you were divorcing her. So I arranged for her to marry one of the young men who were at your party. But my younger daughter is even prettier, and you can have her as your wife."

"This time," Samson answered, "I have a good reason for really hurting some Philistines."

Samson went out and caught three hundred foxes and tied them together in pairs with oil-soaked rags around their tails. Then Samson took the foxes into the Philistine wheat fields that were ready to be harvested. He set the rags on fire and let the foxes go. The wheat fields went up in flames, and so did the stacks of wheat that had already been cut. Even the Philistine vineyards and olive orchards burned.

Some of the Philistines started asking around, "Who could have done such a thing?"

"It was Samson," someone told them. "He married the daughter of that man in Timnah, but then the man gave Samson's wife to one of the men at the wedding."

The Philistine leaders went to Timnah and burned to death Samson's wife and her father.

When Samson found out what they had done, he went to them and said, "You killed them! And I won't rest until I get even with you." Then Samson started hacking them to pieces with his sword.

Samson left Philistia and went to live in the cave at Etam Rock.

The Philistines sent some men from Judah to take Samson captive. But when the Philistines met him, the power of God fell on him and he broke the ropes around his arms. And with a jawbone of a donkey he killed a thousand men.

Samson was a judge in Israel for twenty years.

## Samson in Prison

Judges
16.4-22

Some time later, Samson fell in love with a woman named Delilah, who lived in Sorek Valley. The Philistine rulers went to Delilah and said, "Trick Samson into telling you what makes him so strong and what can make him weak. Then we can tie him up so he can't get away. If you find out his secret, we will each give you eleven hundred pieces of silver."

The next time Samson was at Delilah's house, she asked, "Samson, what makes you so strong? How can I tie you up so you can't get away? Come on, you can tell me."

Samson answered, "If someone ties me up with seven new bowstrings that have never been dried, it will make me just as weak as anyone else."

The Philistine rulers gave seven new bowstrings to Delilah. They also told some of their soldiers to go to Delilah's house and hide in the room where Samson and Delilah were. If the bowstrings made Samson weak, they would be able to capture him.

Delilah tied up Samson with the bowstrings and shouted, "Samson, the Philistines are attacking!"

Samson snapped the bowstrings, as though they were pieces of scorched string. The Philistines had not found out why Samson was so strong.

"You lied and made me look like a fool," Delilah said. "Now tell me. How can I really tie you up?"

Samson answered, "Use some new ropes. If I'm tied up with ropes that have never been used, I'll be just as weak as anyone else."

Delilah got new ropes and again had some Philistines hide in the room. Then she tied up Samson's arms and shouted, "Samson, the Philistines are attacking!"

Samson snapped the ropes as if they were threads.

"You're still lying and making a fool of me," Delilah said. "Tell me how I can tie you up!"

"My hair is in seven braids," Samson replied. "If you weave my braids into the threads on a loom and nail the loom to a wall, then I will be as weak as anyone else."

While Samson was asleep, Delilah wove his braids into the threads on a loom and nailed the loom to a wall. Then she shouted, "Samson, the Philistines are attacking!"

Samson woke up and pulled the loom free from its posts in the ground and from the nails in the wall. Then he pulled his hair free from the woven cloth.

"Samson," Delilah said, "you claim to love me, but you don't mean it! You've made me look like a fool three times now, and you still haven't told me why you are so strong." Delilah started nagging and pestering him day after day, until he couldn't stand it any longer.

Finally, Samson told her the truth. "I have belonged to God ever since I was born, so my hair has never been cut. If it were ever cut off, my strength would leave me, and I would be as weak as anyone else."

Delilah realized that he was telling the truth. So she sent someone to tell the Philistine rulers, "Come to my house one more time. Samson has finally told me the truth."

The Philistine rulers went to Delilah's house, and they brought along the silver they had promised her. Delilah had lulled Samson to sleep with his head resting in her lap. She signaled to one of the Philistine men as she began cutting off Samson's seven braids. And by the time she was finished, Samson's strength was gone. Delilah tied him up and shouted, "Samson, the Philistines are attacking!"

Samson woke up and thought, "I'll break loose and escape, just as I always do." He did not realize that the LORD had stopped helping him.

The Philistines grabbed Samson and poked out his eyes. They took him to the prison in Gaza and chained him up. Then they put him to work, turning a millstone to grind grain. But they didn't cut his hair any more, so it started growing back.

## Samson Dies

Judges
16.23-31

The Philistine rulers threw a big party and sacrificed a lot of animals to their god Dagon. The rulers said:

Samson was our enemy, but our god Dagon
helped us capture him!

Everyone there was having a good time, and they shouted, "Bring out Samson—he's still good for a few more laughs!"

The rulers had Samson brought from the prison, and when the people saw him, this is how they praised their god:

Samson ruined our crops and killed our people.

He was our enemy, but our god
helped us capture him.

They made fun of Samson for a while, then they told him to stand near the columns that supported the roof. A young man was leading Samson by the hand, and Samson said to him, "I need to lean against something. Take me over to the columns that hold up the roof."

The Philistine rulers were celebrating in a temple packed with people and with three thousand more on the flat roof. They had all been watching Samson and making fun of him.

Samson prayed, "Please remember me, LORD God. The Philistines poked out my eyes, but make me strong one last time, so I can take revenge for at least one of my eyes!"

Samson was standing between the two middle columns that held up the roof. He felt around and found one column with his right hand, and the other with his left hand. Then he shouted, "Let me die with the Philistines!" He pushed against the columns as hard as he could, and the temple collapsed with the Philistine rulers and everyone else still inside. Samson killed more Philistines when he died than he had killed during his entire life.

His brothers and the rest of his family went to Gaza and took his body back home. They buried him in his father's tomb, which was located between Zorah and Eshtaol.

Samson was a leader of Israel for twenty years.

# The Prophet Samuel

## Samuel Is Judge in Israel

The last great judge in Israel was called Samuel. He grew up in the temple at Shiloh where he served the LORD and where the LORD appeared to him. The LORD was with him and confirmed every word he said. Everyone in Israel understood that Samuel was chosen to be the LORD's prophet. In Shiloh God revealed his word to Samuel, and Samuel spoke it out to all Israel.

At this time the Israelites were at war with the Philistines. During the first fierce attack the Philistines killed about four thousand men on the battlefield. They captured the sacred chest where the LORD's agreement with Israel was kept, but they suffered great disasters so they sent it back. The chest was put in Kiriath-Jearim, which is also called Baalah.

The Israelites suffered twenty years under the Philistine rule. Samuel told the people of Israel: "If you really want to turn back to the LORD, then prove it. Get rid of your foreign idols, including the ones of the goddess Astarte. Turn to the LORD with all your heart and worship only him. Then he will rescue you from the Philistines." The people obeyed, and when the Philistines attacked again, the LORD helped the Israelites, and the Philistines suffered a great defeat. After this there was peace as long as Samuel lived.

## Saul Is Chosen as King

When Samuel was old, the elders of Israel demanded that he choose a king to govern them just as the other nations had. This did not please Samuel, but when he asked the LORD about it, the LORD told him to give the people what they wanted.

Kish was a wealthy man who belonged to the tribe of Benjamin. His father was Abiel, his grandfather was Zeror, his great-grandfather was Becorath, and his great-great-grandfather was Aphiah. Kish had a son named Saul, who was better looking and more than a head taller than anyone else in all Israel.

The day before Saul came, the LORD had told Samuel, "I've seen how my people are suffering, and I've heard their call for help. About this time tomorrow I'll send you a man from the tribe of Benjamin, who will rescue my people from the Philistines. I want you to pour olive oil on his head to show that he will be their leader."

Samuel looked at Saul, and the LORD told Samuel, "This is the man I told you about. He's the one who will rule Israel."

The next morning when Saul and his servant were about to leave, Samuel joined them. They had almost reached the edge of town when Samuel stopped and said, "Have your servant go on. Stay here with me for a few minutes, and I'll tell you what God has told me."

After the servant had gone, Samuel took a small jar of olive oil and poured it on Saul's head. Then he kissed Saul and told him:

The LORD has chosen you to be the leader and ruler of his people.

Samuel sent messengers to tell the Israelites to come to Mizpah and meet with the LORD. When everyone had arrived, Samuel said:

The LORD God of Israel told me to remind you that he had rescued you from the Egyptians and from the other nations that abused you.

God has rescued you from your troubles and hard times. But you have rejected your God and have asked for a king. Now each tribe and clan must come near the place of worship so the LORD can choose a king.

Samuel brought each tribe, one after the other, to the altar, and the LORD chose the Benjamin tribe. Next, Samuel brought each clan of Benjamin there, and the LORD chose the Matri clan. Finally, Saul the son of Kish was chosen. But when they looked for him, he was nowhere to be found.

The people prayed, "Our LORD, is Saul here?"

"Yes," the LORD answered, "he is hiding behind the baggage."

The people ran and got Saul and brought him into the middle of the crowd. He was more than a head taller than anyone else. "Look closely at the man the LORD has chosen!" Samuel told the crowd. "There is no one like him!"

The crowd shouted, "Long live the king!"

Samuel explained the rights and duties of a king and wrote them all in a book. He put the book in a temple building at one of the places where the LORD was worshiped. Then Samuel sent everyone home.

God had encouraged some young men to become followers of Saul, and when he returned to his hometown of Gibeah, they went with him. But some worthless fools said, "How can someone like Saul rescue us from our enemies?" They did not want Saul to be their king, and so they didn't bring him any gifts. But Saul kept calm.

## Saul Does Not Obey the LORD

1 Samuel 14.47,48

When Saul became king, the Moabites, the Ammonites, the Edomites, the kings of Zobah, the Philistines, and the Amalekites had all been robbing the Israelites. Saul fought back against these enemies and stopped them from robbing Israel. He was a brave commander and always won his battles.

But gradually he did not consider it so necessary to obey the LORD's commands.

1 Samuel 15.10,11

The LORD told Samuel, "Saul has stopped obeying me, and I'm sorry that I made him king."

Samuel was angry, and he cried out in prayer to the LORD all night.

The next morning Samuel went to Saul and said:

1 Samuel 15.23

"Rebelling against God or disobeying him because you are proud is just as bad as worshiping idols or asking them for advice. You refused to do what God told you, so God has decided that you can't be king."

1 Samuel 15.34,35a

Samuel went home to Ramah, and Saul returned to his home in Gibeah. Even though Samuel felt sad about Saul, Samuel never saw him again.

102

# King David

## *Samuel Anoints David as King*

1 Samuel
16.1

One day the LORD said, "Samuel, I've rejected Saul, and I refuse to let him be king any longer. Stop feeling sad about him. Put some olive oil in a small container and go visit a man named Jesse, who lives in Bethlehem. I've chosen one of his sons to be my king."

1 Samuel
16.4-13

Samuel did what the LORD told him and went to Bethlehem. The town leaders went to meet him, but they were terribly afraid and asked, "Is this a friendly visit?"

"Yes, it is!" Samuel answered. "I've come to offer a sacrifice to the LORD. Get yourselves ready to take part in the sacrifice and come with me." Samuel also invited Jesse and his sons to come to the sacrifice, and he got them ready to take part.

When Jesse and his sons arrived, Samuel noticed Jesse's oldest son, Eliab. "He has to be the one the LORD has chosen," Samuel said to himself.

But the LORD told him, "Samuel, don't think Eliab is the one just because he's tall and handsome. He isn't the one I've chosen. People judge others by what they look like, but I judge people by what is in their hearts."

Jesse told his son Abinadab to go over to Samuel, but Samuel said, "No, the LORD hasn't chosen him."

Next, Jesse sent his son Shammah to him, and Samuel said, "The LORD hasn't chosen him either."

Jesse had all seven of his sons go over to Samuel. Finally, Samuel said, "Jesse, the LORD hasn't chosen any of these young men. Do you have any more sons?"

"Yes," Jesse answered. "My youngest son David is out taking care of the sheep."

"Send for him!" Samuel said. "We won't start the ceremony until he gets here."

Jesse sent for David. He was a healthy, good-looking boy with a sparkle in his eyes. As soon as David came, the LORD told Samuel, "He's the one! Get up and pour the olive oil on his head."

Samuel poured the oil on David's head while his brothers watched. At that moment, the Spirit of the LORD took control of David and stayed with him from then on.

Samuel returned home to Ramah.

## David Comes to Saul's Court

1 Samuel
16.14-23

The Spirit of the LORD had left Saul, and an evil spirit from the LORD was terrifying him. "It's an evil spirit from God that's frightening you," Saul's officials told him. "Your Majesty, let us go and look for someone who is good at playing the harp. He can play for you whenever the evil spirit from God bothers you, and you'll feel better."

"All right," Saul answered. "Find me someone who is good at playing the harp and bring him here."

"A man named Jesse who lives in Bethlehem has a son who can play the harp," one official said. "He's a brave warrior, he's good-looking, he can speak well, and the LORD is with him."

Saul sent a message to Jesse: "Tell your son David to leave your sheep and come here to me."

Jesse loaded a donkey with bread and a goatskin full of wine, then he told David to take the donkey and a young goat to Saul. David went to Saul and started working for him. Saul liked him so much that he put David in charge of carrying his weapons. Not long after this, Saul sent another message to Jesse: "I really like David. Please let him stay with me."

Whenever the evil spirit from God bothered Saul, David would play his harp. Saul would relax and feel better, and the evil spirit would go away.

## David and Goliath

1 Samuel
17.1-11

The Philistines got ready for war and brought their troops together to attack the town of Socoh in Judah. They set up camp at Ephes-Dammim, between Socoh and Azekah. King Saul and the Israelite army set up camp on a hill overlooking Elah Valley, and they got ready to fight the Philistine army that was on a hill on the other side of the valley.

The Philistine army had a hero named Goliath who was from the town of Gath and was over nine feet tall. He wore a bronze helmet and had bronze armor to protect his chest and legs. The chest armor alone weighed about one hundred twenty-five pounds. He carried a bronze sword strapped on his back, and his spear was so big that the iron spearhead alone weighed more than fifteen pounds. A soldier always walked in front of Goliath to carry his shield.

Goliath went out and shouted to the army of Israel:

Why are you lining up for battle? I'm the best soldier in our army, and all of you are in Saul's army. Choose your best soldier to come out and fight me! If he can kill me, our people will be your slaves. But if I kill him, your people will be our slaves. Here and now I challenge Israel's whole army! Choose someone to fight me!

Saul and his men heard what Goliath said, but they were so frightened of Goliath that they couldn't do a thing.

Goliath came out and gave his challenge every morning and every evening for forty days.

One day, Jesse told David, "Hurry and take this sack of roasted grain and these ten loaves of bread to your brothers at the army camp. And here are ten large chunks of cheese to take to their commanding officer. Find out how your brothers are doing and bring back something that shows that they're all right. They're with Saul's army, fighting the Philistines in Elah Valley."

David obeyed his father. He got up early the next morning and left someone else in charge of the sheep; then he loaded the supplies and started off. He reached the army camp just as the soldiers were taking their places and shouting the battle cry. The army of Israel and the Philistine army stood there facing each other.

David left his things with the man in charge of supplies and ran up to the battle line to ask his brothers if they were well. While David was talking with them, Goliath came out from the line of Philistines and started boasting as usual. David heard him.

When the Israelite soldiers saw Goliath, they were scared and ran off. They said to each other, "Look how he keeps coming out to insult us. The king is offering a big reward to the man who kills Goliath. That man will even get to marry the king's daughter, and no one in his family will ever have to pay taxes again."

David asked some soldiers standing nearby, "What will a man get for killing this Philistine and stopping him from insulting our people? Who does that worthless Philistine think he is? He's making fun of the army of the living God!"

The soldiers told David what the king would give the man who killed Goliath.

## David Defeats Goliath

1 Samuel
17.31-54

Some soldiers overheard David talking, so they told Saul what David had said. Saul sent for David, and David came. "Your Majesty," he said, "this Philistine shouldn't turn us into cowards. I'll go out and fight him myself!"

"You don't have a chance against him," Saul replied. "You're only a boy, and he's been a soldier all his life."

But David told him:

Your Majesty, I take care of my father's sheep. And when one of them is dragged off by a lion or a bear, I go after it and beat the wild animal until it lets the sheep go. If the wild animal turns and attacks me, I grab it by the throat and kill it.

Sir, I have killed lions and bears that way, and I can kill this worthless Philistine. He shouldn't have made fun of the army of the living God! The LORD has rescued me from the claws of lions and bears, and he will keep me safe from the hands of this Philistine.

"All right," Saul answered, "go ahead and fight him. And I hope the LORD will help you."

Saul had his own military clothes and armor put on David, and he gave David a bronze helmet to wear. David strapped on a sword and tried to walk around, but he was not used to wearing those things.

"I can't move with all this stuff on," David said. "I'm just not used to it."

David took off the armor and picked up his shepherd's stick. He went out to a stream and picked up five smooth rocks and put them in his leather bag. Then with his sling in his hand, he went straight toward Goliath.

Goliath came toward David, walking behind the soldier who was carrying his shield. When Goliath saw that David was just a healthy, good-looking boy, he made fun of him. "Do you think I'm a dog?" Goliath asked. "Is that why you've come after me with a stick?" He cursed David in the name of the Philistine gods and shouted, "Come on! When I'm finished with you, I'll feed you to the birds and wild animals!"

David answered:

You've come out to fight me with a sword and a spear and a dagger. But I've come out to fight you in the name of the LORD All-Powerful. He is the God of Israel's army, and you have insulted him too!

Today the LORD will help me defeat you. I'll knock you down and cut off your head, and I'll feed the bodies of the other Philistine soldiers to the birds and wild animals. Then the whole world will know that Israel has a real God. Everybody here will see that the LORD doesn't need swords or spears to save his people. The LORD always wins his battles, and he will help us defeat you.

When Goliath started forward, David ran toward him. He put a rock in his sling and swung the sling around by its straps. When he let go of one strap, the rock flew out and hit Goliath on the forehead. It cracked his skull, and he fell facedown on the ground. David defeated Goliath with a sling and a rock. He killed him without even using a sword.

David ran over and pulled out Goliath's sword. Then he used it to cut off Goliath's head.

When the Philistines saw what had happened to their hero, they started running away. But the soldiers of Israel and Judah let out a battle cry and went after them as far as Gath and Ekron. The bodies of the Philistines were scattered all along the road from Shaaraim to Gath and Ekron.

When the Israelite army returned from chasing the Philistines, they took what they wanted from the enemy camp. David took Goliath's head to Jerusalem, but he kept Goliath's weapons in his own tent.

## Saul's Son Jonathan and David Become Friends

1 Samuel
18.2-5

From that time on, Saul kept David in his service and would not let David go back to his own family.

Jonathan liked David so much that they promised to always be loyal friends. Jonathan took off the robe that he was wearing and gave it to David. He also gave him his military clothes, his sword, his bow and arrows, and his belt.

David was a success in everything that Saul sent him to do, and Saul made him a high officer in his army. That pleased everyone, including Saul's other officers.

## Saul Becomes Jealous of David

1 Samuel
18.6-16

David had killed Goliath, the battle was over, and the Israelite army set out for home. As the army went along, women came out of each Israelite town to welcome King Saul. They were singing happy songs and dancing to the music of tambourines and harps. They sang:

Saul has killed a thousand enemies;

David has killed ten thousand enemies!

This song made Saul very angry, and he thought, "They are saying that David has killed ten times more enemies than I ever did. Next they will want to make him king." Saul never again trusted David.

The next day the LORD let an evil spirit take control of Saul, and he began acting like a crazy man inside his house. David came to play the harp for Saul as usual, but this time Saul had a spear in his hand. Saul thought, "I'll pin David to the wall." He threw the spear at David twice, but David dodged and got away both times.

Saul was afraid of David, because the LORD was helping David and was no longer helping him. Saul put David in charge of a thousand soldiers and sent him out to fight. The LORD helped David, and he and his soldiers always won their battles. This made Saul even more afraid of David. But everyone else in Judah and Israel was loyal to David, because he led the army in battle.

1 Samuel
19.1,2

One day, Saul told his son Jonathan and his officers to kill David. But Jonathan liked David a lot, and he warned David, "My father is trying to have you killed, so be very careful."

111

## David and Jonathan

1 Samuel
20.17-24a

Jonathan thought as much of David as he did of himself, so he asked David to promise once more that he would be a loyal friend. After this Jonathan said:

> Tomorrow is the New Moon Festival, and people will wonder where you are, because your place will be empty. By the day after tomorrow, everyone will think you've been gone a long time. Then go to the place where you hid before and stay beside Going-Away Rock. I'll shoot three arrows at a target off to the side of the rock, and send my servant to find the arrows.
>
> You'll know if it's safe to come out by what I tell him. If it is safe, I swear by the living LORD that I'll say, "The arrows are on this side of you! Pick them up!" But if it isn't safe, I'll say to the boy, "The arrows are farther away!" This will mean that the LORD wants you to leave, and you must go. But he will always watch us to make sure that we keep the promise we made to each other.

So David hid there in the field.

1 Samuel
20.27-42

The day after the New Moon Festival, when David's place was still empty, Saul asked Jonathan, "Why hasn't that son of Jesse come to eat with us? He wasn't here yesterday, and he still isn't here today!"

112

Jonathan answered, "The reason David hasn't come to eat with you is that he begged me to let him go to Bethlehem. He said, 'Please let me go. My family is offering a sacrifice, and my brother told me I have to be there. Do me this favor and let me slip away to see my brothers.' "

Saul was furious with Jonathan and yelled, "You're no son of mine, you traitor! I know you've chosen to be loyal to that son of Jesse. You should be ashamed of yourself! And your own mother should be ashamed that you were ever born. You'll never be safe, and your kingdom will be in danger as long as that son of Jesse is alive. Turn him over to me now! He deserves to die!"

"Why do you want to kill David?" Jonathan asked. "What has he done?"

Saul threw his spear at Jonathan and tried to kill him. Then Jonathan was sure that his father really did want to kill David. Jonathan was angry that his father had insulted David so terribly. He got up, left the table, and didn't eat anything all that day.

In the morning, Jonathan went out to the field to meet David. He took a servant boy along and told him, "When I shoot the arrows, you run and find them for me."

The boy started running, and Jonathan shot an arrow so that it would go beyond him. When the boy got near the place where the arrow had landed, Jonathan shouted, "Isn't the arrow on past you?" Jonathan shouted to him again, "Hurry up! Don't stop!"

The boy picked up the arrows and brought them back to Jonathan, but he had no idea about what was going on. Only Jonathan and David knew. Jonathan gave his weapons to the boy and told him, "Take these back into town."

After the boy had gone, David got up from beside the mound and bowed very low three times. Then he and Jonathan kissed each other and cried, but David cried louder. Jonathan said, "Take care of yourself. And remember, we each have asked the LORD to watch and make sure that we and our descendants keep our promise forever."

David left and Jonathan went back to town.

# David and Saul in the Desert

1 Samuel
23.14
1 Samuel
24.1-13

David stayed in hideouts in the hill country of Ziph Desert. Saul kept searching, but God never let Saul catch him.

When Saul got back from fighting off the Philistines, he heard that David was in the desert around En-Gedi. Saul led three thousand of Israel's best soldiers out to look for David and his men near Wild Goat Rocks at En-Gedi. There were some sheep pens along the side of the road, and one of them was built around the entrance to a cave. Saul went into the cave to relieve himself.

David and his men were hiding at the back of the cave. They whispered to David, "The LORD told you he was going to let you defeat your enemies and do whatever you want with them. This must be the day the LORD was talking about."

David sneaked over and cut off a small piece of Saul's robe, but Saul didn't notice a thing. Afterwards, David was sorry that he had even done that, and he told his men, "Stop talking foolishly. We're not going to attack Saul. He's my king, and I pray that the LORD will keep me from doing anything to harm his chosen king."

Saul left the cave and started down the road. Soon, David also got up and left the cave. "Your Majesty!" he shouted from a distance.

Saul turned around to look. David bowed down very low and said:

Your Majesty, why do you listen to people who say that I'm trying to harm you? You can see for yourself that the LORD gave me the chance to catch you in the cave today. Some of my men wanted to kill you, but I wouldn't let them do it. I told them, "I will not harm the LORD's chosen king!" Your Majesty, look at what I'm holding. You can see that it's a piece of your robe. If I could cut off a piece of your robe, I could have killed you. But I let you live, and that should prove I'm not trying to harm you or to rebel. I haven't done anything to you, and yet you keep trying to ambush and kill me.

I'll let the LORD decide which one of us has done right. I pray that the LORD will punish you for what you're doing to me, but I won't do anything to you. An old proverb says, "Only evil people do evil things," and so I won't harm you.

## Samuel Dies

1 Samuel
25.1

Samuel died, and people from all over Israel gathered to mourn for him when he was buried at his home in Ramah. Meanwhile, David moved his camp to Paran Desert.

## Saul Dies

1 Samuel
31.1-6

Meanwhile, the Philistines were fighting Israel at Mount Gilboa. Israel's soldiers ran from the Philistines, and many of them were killed. The Philistines closed in on Saul and his sons, and they killed his sons Jonathan, Abinadab, and Malchishua. The fighting was fierce around Saul, and he was badly wounded by enemy arrows.

Saul told the soldier who carried his weapons, "Kill me with your sword! I don't want those worthless Philistines to torture me and make fun." But the soldier was afraid to kill him.

Saul then took out his own sword; he stuck the blade into his stomach, and fell on it. When the soldier knew that Saul was dead, he killed himself in the same way.

Saul was dead, his three sons were dead, and the soldier who carried his weapons was dead. They and all his soldiers died on that same day.

# David Becomes King of Israel

2 Samuel
5.1-10

Israel's leaders met with David at Hebron and said, "We are your relatives. Even when Saul was king, you led our nation in battle. And the LORD promised that someday you would rule Israel and take care of us like a shepherd."

During the meeting, David made an agreement with the leaders and asked the LORD to be their witness. Then the leaders poured olive oil on David's head to show that he was now the king of Israel.

David was thirty years old when he became king, and he ruled for forty years. He lived in Hebron for the first seven and a half years and ruled only Judah. Then he moved to Jerusalem, where he ruled both Israel and Judah for thirty-three years.

The Jebusites lived in Jerusalem, and David led his army there to attack them. The Jebusites did not think he could get in, so they told him, "You can't get in here! We could run you off, even if we couldn't see or walk!"

David told his troops, "You will have to go up through the water tunnel to get those Jebusites. I hate people like them who can't walk or see."

That's why there is still a rule that says, "Only people who can walk and see are allowed in the temple."

David captured the fortress on Mount Zion, then he moved there and named it David's City. He had the city rebuilt, starting with the landfill to the east. David became a great and strong ruler, because the LORD All-Powerful was on his side.

# David Brings the Sacred Chest to Jerusalem

2 Samuel
6.1-15

David brought together thirty thousand of Israel's best soldiers and led them to Baalah in Judah, which was also called Kiriath-Jearim. They were going there to get the sacred chest and bring it back to Jerusalem. The throne of the LORD All-Powerful is above the winged creatures on top of this chest, and he is worshiped there.

They put the sacred chest on a new ox cart and started bringing it down the hill from Abinadab's house. Abinadab's sons Uzzah and Ahio were guiding the ox cart, with Ahio walking in front of it.

Some of the people of Israel were playing music on small harps and other stringed instruments, and on tambourines, castanets, and cymbals. David and the others were happy, and they danced for the LORD with all their might.

But when they came to Nacon's threshing-floor, the oxen stumbled, so Uzzah reached out and took hold of the sacred chest. The LORD God was very angry at Uzzah for doing this, and he killed Uzzah right there beside the chest.

David got angry at God for killing Uzzah. He named that place "Bursting Out Against Uzzah," and that's what it's still called.

David was afraid of the LORD and thought, "Should I really take the sacred chest to my city?" He decided not to take it there. Instead, he turned off the road and took it to the home of Obed Edom, who was from Gath.

The chest stayed there for three months, and the LORD greatly blessed Obed Edom, his family, and everything he owned. Then someone told King David, "The LORD has done this because the sacred chest is in Obed Edom's house."

Right away, David went to Obed Edom's house to get the chest and bring it to David's City. Everyone was celebrating. The people carrying the chest walked six steps, then David sacrificed an ox and a choice cow. He was dancing for the LORD with all his might, but he wore only a linen cloth. He and everyone else were celebrating by shouting and blowing horns while the chest was being carried along.

## God's Promises to David and His Family

2 Samuel

7.1-5

King David moved into his new palace, and the LORD let his kingdom be at peace. Then one day, as David was talking with Nathan the prophet, David said, "Look around! I live in a palace made of cedar, but the sacred chest has to stay in a tent."

Nathan replied, "The LORD is with you, so do what you want!"

That night, the LORD told Nathan to go to David and give him this message:

> David, you are my servant, so listen to what I say. Why should you build a temple for me?

118

I'll choose one of your sons to be king when you reach the end of your life and are buried in the tomb of your ancestors. I'll make him a strong ruler, and no one will be able to take his kingdom away from him. He will be the one to build a temple for me. I will be his father, and he will be my son.

When he does wrong, I'll see that he is corrected, just as children are corrected by their parents. But I will never put an end to my agreement with him, as I put an end to my agreement with Saul, who was king before you. I will make sure that one of your descendants will always be king.

Nathan told David exactly what he had heard in the vision.

## David and Bathsheba

It was now spring, the time when kings go to war. David sent out the whole Israelite army under the command of Joab and his officers. They destroyed the Ammonite army and surrounded the capital city of Rabbah, but David stayed in Jerusalem.

Late one afternoon, David got up from a nap and was walking around on the flat roof of his palace. A beautiful young woman was down below in her courtyard, bathing as her religion required. David happened to see her, and he sent one of his servants to find out who she was.

The servant came back and told David, "Her name is Bathsheba. She is the daughter of Eliam, and she is the wife of Uriah the Hittite."

David sent some messengers to bring her to his palace. She came to him, and he slept with her. Then she returned home. But later, when she found out that she was going to have a baby, she sent someone to David with this message: "I'm pregnant!"

David sent a message to Joab: "Send Uriah the Hittite to me."

Early the next morning, David wrote a letter and told Uriah to deliver it to Joab. The letter said: "Put Uriah on the front line where the fighting is the worst. Then pull the troops back from him, so that he will be wounded and die."

Joab had been carefully watching the city of Rabbah, and he put Uriah in a place where he knew there were some of the enemy's best soldiers. When the men of the city came out, they fought and killed some of David's soldiers—Uriah the Hittite was one of them.

2 Samuel
11.26,27a

When Bathsheba heard that her husband was dead, she mourned for him. Then after the time for mourning was over, David sent someone to bring her to the palace. She became David's wife, and they had a son.

## The Prophet Nathan Speaks to David

2 Samuel
11.27b—12.9

The LORD was angry at what David had done, and he sent Nathan the prophet to tell this story to David:

A rich man and a poor man lived in the same town. The rich man owned a lot of sheep and cattle, but the poor man had only one little lamb that he had bought and raised. The lamb became a pet for him and his children. He even let it eat from his plate and drink from his cup and sleep on his lap. The lamb was like one of his own children.

One day someone came to visit the rich man, but the rich man didn't want to kill any of his own sheep or cattle and serve it to the visitor. So he stole the poor man's little lamb and served it instead.

David was furious with the rich man and said to Nathan, "I swear by the living LORD that the man who did this deserves to die! And because he didn't have any pity on the poor man, he will have to pay four times what the lamb was worth."

Then Nathan told David:

You are that rich man! Now listen to what the LORD God of Israel says to you: "I chose you to be the king of Israel. I kept you safe from Saul and even gave you his house and his wives. I let you rule Israel and Judah, and if that had not been enough, I would have given you much more. Why did you disobey me and do such a horrible thing? You murdered Uriah the Hittite by having the Ammonites kill him, so you could take his wife.

2 Samuel
12.13-25

David said, "I have disobeyed the LORD."

"Yes, you have!" Nathan answered. "You showed you didn't care what the LORD wanted. He has forgiven you, and you won't die. But your newborn son will." Then Nathan went back home.

The LORD made David's young son very sick.

So David went without eating to show his sorrow, and he begged God to make the boy well. David would not sleep on his bed, but spent each night lying on the floor. His officials stood beside him and tried to talk him into getting up. But he would not get up or eat with them.

After the child had been sick for seven days, he died, but the officials were afraid to tell David. They said to each other, "Even when the boy was alive, David wouldn't listen to us. How can we tell him his son is dead? He might do something terrible!"

David noticed his servants whispering, and he knew the boy was dead. "Did my son die?" he asked his servants.

"Yes, he did," they answered.

David got up off the floor; he took a bath, combed his hair, and dressed. He went into the LORD's tent and worshiped, then he went back home. David asked for something to eat, and when his servants brought him some food, he ate it.

His officials said, "What are you doing? You went without eating and cried for your son while he was alive! But now that he's dead, you're up and eating."

David answered:

While he was still alive, I went without food and cried because there was still hope. I said to myself, "Who knows? Maybe the LORD will have pity on me and let the child live." But now that he's dead, why should I go without eating? I can't bring him back! Someday I will join him in death, but he can't return to me.

David comforted his wife Bathsheba and slept with her. Later on, she gave birth to another son and named him Solomon. The LORD loved Solomon and sent Nathan the prophet to tell David, "The LORD will call him Jedidiah."

After this King David faced many dangerous situations. Enemies sought to kill him and he had to flee to the desert. Afterwards he also was at war with the Philistines. But God saved him from all his enemies.

# King Solomon

## Solomon Becomes King

*King David had many sons, but it was Solomon who succeeded him as king.*

1 Kings
1.32-40

David said, "Tell Zadok, Nathan, and Benaiah to come here."

When they arrived, he told them:

Take along some of my officials and have Solomon ride my own mule to Gihon Spring. When you get there, Zadok and Nathan will make Solomon the new king of Israel. Then after the ceremony is over, have someone blow a trumpet and tell everyone to shout, "Long live King Solomon!" Bring him back here, and he will take my place as king. He is the one I have chosen to rule Israel and Judah.

Benaiah answered, "We will do it, Your Majesty. I pray that the LORD your God will let it happen. The LORD has always watched over you, and I pray that he will now watch over Solomon. May the LORD help Solomon to be an even greater king than you."

Zadok, Nathan, and Benaiah left and took along the two groups of David's special bodyguards. Solomon rode on David's mule as they led him to Gihon Spring. Zadok the priest brought some olive oil from the sacred tent and poured it on Solomon's head to show that he was now king. A trumpet was blown and everyone shouted, "Long live King Solomon!" Then they played flutes and celebrated as they followed Solomon back to Jerusalem. They made so much noise that the ground shook.

1 Kings
2.10-12

David was king of Israel forty years. He ruled seven years from Hebron and thirty-three years from Jerusalem. Then he died and was buried in Jerusalem. His son Solomon became king and took control of David's kingdom.

## Solomon's Dream

1 Kings
3.5-15

One night while Solomon was in Gibeon, the LORD God appeared to him in a dream and said, "Solomon, ask for anything you want, and I will give it to you."

Solomon answered:

My father David, your servant, was honest and did what you commanded. You were always loyal to him, and you gave him a son who is now king. LORD God, I'm your servant, and you've made me king in my father's place. But I'm very young and know so little about being a leader. And now I must rule your chosen people, even though there are too many of them to count.

Please make me wise and teach me the difference between right and wrong. Then I will know how to rule your people. If you don't, there is no way I could rule this great nation of yours.

God said:

Solomon, I'm pleased that you asked for this. You could have asked to live a long time or to be rich. Or you could have asked for your enemies to be destroyed. Instead, you asked for wisdom to make right decisions. So I'll make you wiser than anyone who has ever lived or ever will live.

I'll also give you what you didn't ask for. You'll be rich and respected as long as you live, and you'll be greater than any other king. If you obey me and follow my commands, as your father David did, I'll let you live a long time.

Solomon woke up and realized that God had spoken to him in the dream. He went back to Jerusalem and stood in front of the sacred chest, where he offered sacrifices to please the Lord and sacrifices to ask his blessing. Then Solomon gave a feast for his officials.

## Solomon Makes a Difficult Decision

1 Kings
3.16-28

One day two women came to King Solomon, and one of them said:

Your Majesty, this woman and I live in the same house. Not long ago my baby was born at home, and three days later her baby was born. Nobody else was there with us.

One night while we were all asleep, she rolled over on her baby, and he died. Then while I was still asleep, she got up and took my son out of my bed. She put him in her bed, then she put her dead baby next to me.

In the morning when I got up to feed my son, I saw that he was dead. But when I looked at him in the light, I knew he wasn't my son.

"No!" the other woman shouted. "He was your son. My baby is alive!"

"The dead baby is yours," the first woman yelled. "Mine is alive!"

They argued back and forth in front of Solomon, until finally he said, "Both of you say this live baby is yours. Someone bring me a sword."

A sword was brought, and Solomon ordered, "Cut the baby in half! That way each of you can have part of him."

"Please don't kill my son," the baby's mother screamed. "Your Majesty, I love him very much, but give him to her. Just don't kill him."

The other woman shouted, "Go ahead and cut him in half. Then neither of us will have the baby."

Solomon said, "Don't kill the baby." Then he pointed to the first woman, "She is his real mother. Give the baby to her."

Everyone in Israel was amazed when they heard how Solomon had made his decision. They realized that God had given him wisdom to judge fairly.

124

The LORD had granted peace in the land. And Solomon wanted to build a temple that would be the LORD's house. He had it built with the best and finest materials he could find. The inside of it was covered with gold. Deep inside the temple was a room that was called the most holy place. The sacred chest was placed there. All the objects in the temple were covered with gold or bronze.

When the temple was ready, Solomon had the sacred chest brought from Zion. Solomon knelt before the LORD, raised up his hands toward heaven and prayed to God. He stood up and blessed the people of Israel.

That day Solomon and the people of Israel offered many sacrifices to the LORD and thus they dedicated the temple.

## The Queen of Sheba Visits Solomon

1 Kings 10.1-9

The Queen of Sheba heard how famous Solomon was, so she went to Jerusalem to test him with difficult questions. She took along several of her officials, and she loaded her camels with gifts of spices, jewels, and gold. When she arrived, she and Solomon talked about everything she could think of. He answered every question, no matter how difficult it was.

The Queen was amazed at Solomon's wisdom. She was breathless when she saw his palace, the food on his table, his officials, his servants in their uniforms, the people who served his food, and the sacrifices he offered at the LORD's temple. She said:

Solomon, in my own country I had heard about your wisdom and all you've done. But I didn't believe it until I saw it with my own eyes! And there's so much I didn't hear about. You are wiser and richer than I was told. Your wives and officials are lucky to be here where they can listen to the wise things you say.

I praise the LORD your God. He is pleased with you and has made you king of Israel. The LORD loves Israel, so he has given them a king who will rule fairly and honestly.

126

## The Nation Is Divided

1 Kings
11.42,43

After Solomon had ruled forty years from Jerusalem, he died and was buried there in the city of his father David. His son Rehoboam then became king.

After Solomon's death the large kingdom was divided. Rehoboam became the king of Judah in the south. Jeroboam became king of the ten tribes of Israel in the north. Both in Judah and Israel people worshiped pagan gods, most often Baal and Astarte. Rehoboam, Jeroboam, and most of the succeeding kings did not obey the LORD's commands, and did evil in the eyes of the LORD. One of these kings was Ahab. He worshiped idols and oppressed the poor.

# The Prophet Elijah

### The LORD Takes Care of Elijah

1 Kings
17.1-7

Elijah was a prophet from Tishbe in Gilead. One day he went to King Ahab and said, "I'm a servant of the living LORD, the God of Israel. And I swear in his name that it won't rain until I say so. There won't even be any dew on the ground."

Later, the LORD said to Elijah, "Leave and go across the Jordan River so you can hide near Cherith Creek. You can drink water from the creek, and eat the food I've told the ravens to bring you."

Elijah obeyed the LORD and went to live near Cherith Creek. Ravens brought him bread and meat twice a day, and he drank water from the creek. But after a while, it dried up because there was no rain.

### Elijah and the Widow of Zarephath

1 Kings
17.8-24

The LORD told Elijah, "Go to the town of Zarephath in Sidon and live there. I've told a widow in that town to give you food."

When Elijah came near the town gate of Zarephath, he saw a widow gathering sticks for a fire. "Would you please bring me a cup of water?" he asked. As she left to get it, he asked, "Would you also please bring me a piece of bread?"

The widow answered, "In the name of the living LORD your God, I swear that I don't have any bread. All I have is a handful of flour and a little olive oil. I'm on my way home now with these few sticks to cook what I have for my son and me. After that, we will starve to death."

Elijah said, "Everything will be fine. Do what you said. Go home and fix something for you and your son. But first, please make a small piece of bread and bring it to me. The LORD God of Israel has promised that your jar of flour won't run out and your bottle of oil won't dry up before he sends rain for the crops."

The widow went home and did exactly what Elijah had told her. She and Elijah and her family had enough food for a long time. The LORD kept the promise that his prophet Elijah had made, and she did not run out of flour or oil.

Several days later, the son of the woman who owned the house got sick, and he kept getting worse, until finally he died.

The woman shouted at Elijah, "What have I done to you? I thought you were God's prophet. Did you come here to cause the death of my son as a reminder that I've sinned against God?"

"Bring me your son," Elijah said. Then he took the boy from her arms and carried him upstairs to the room where he was staying. Elijah laid the boy on his bed and prayed, "LORD God, why did you do such a terrible thing to this woman? She's letting me stay here, and now you've let her son die." Elijah stretched himself out over the boy three times, while praying, "LORD God, bring this boy back to life!"

The LORD answered Elijah's prayer, and the boy started breathing again. Elijah picked him up and carried him downstairs. He gave the boy to his mother and said, "Look, your son is alive."

"You are God's prophet!" the woman replied. "Now I know that you really do speak for the LORD."

## Elijah on Mount Carmel

1 Kings
18.1,2

1 Kings
18.17-46

For three years no rain fell in Samaria, and there was almost nothing to eat anywhere. The LORD said to Elijah, "Go and meet with King Ahab. I will soon make it rain." So Elijah went to see Ahab.

When he saw him, Ahab shouted, "There you are, the biggest troublemaker in Israel!"

Elijah answered:

You're the troublemaker—not me! You and your family have disobeyed the LORD's commands by worshiping Baal.

Call together everyone from Israel and have them meet me on Mount Carmel. Be sure to bring along the four hundred fifty prophets of Baal and the four hundred prophets of Asherah who eat at Jezebel's table.

Ahab got everyone together, then they went to meet Elijah on Mount Carmel. Elijah stood in front of them and said, "How much longer will you try to have things both ways? If the LORD is God, worship him! But if Baal is God, worship him!"

The people did not say a word.

Then Elijah continued:

I am the LORD's only prophet, but Baal has four hundred fifty prophets.

Bring us two bulls. Baal's prophets can take one of them, kill it, and cut it into pieces. Then they can put the meat on the wood without lighting the fire. I will do the same thing with the other bull, and I won't light a fire under it either.

The prophets of Baal will pray to their god, and I will pray to the LORD. The one who answers by starting the fire is God.

"That's a good idea," everyone agreed.

Elijah said to Baal's prophets, "There are more of you, so you go first. Pick out a bull and get it ready, but don't light the fire. Then pray to your god."

They chose their bull, then they got it ready and prayed to Baal all morning, asking him to start the fire. They danced around the altar and shouted, "Answer us, Baal!" But there was no answer.

At noon, Elijah began making fun of them. "Pray louder!" he said. "Baal must be a god. Maybe he's day-dreaming or using the toilet or traveling somewhere. Or maybe he's asleep, and you have to wake him up."

The prophets kept shouting louder and louder, and they cut themselves with swords and knives until they were bleeding. This was the way they worshiped, and they kept it up all afternoon. But there was no answer of any kind.

Elijah told everyone to gather around him while he repaired the LORD's altar. Then he used twelve stones to build an altar in honor of the LORD. Each stone stood for one of the tribes of Israel, which was the name the LORD had given to their ancestor Jacob. Elijah dug a ditch around the altar, large enough to hold about thirteen quarts. He placed the wood on the altar, then they cut the bull into pieces and laid the meat on the wood.

He told the people, "Fill four large jars with water and pour it over the meat and the wood." After they did this, he told them to do it two more times. They did exactly as he said until finally, the water ran down the altar and filled the ditch.

When it was time for the evening sacrifice, Elijah prayed:

Our LORD, you are the God of Abraham, Isaac, and Israel. Now, prove that you are the God of this nation, and that I, your servant, have done this at your command. Please answer me, so these people will know that you are the LORD God, and that you will turn their hearts back to you.

The LORD immediately sent fire, and it burned up the sacrifice, the wood, and the stones. It scorched the ground everywhere around the altar and dried up every drop of water in the ditch.

When the crowd saw what had happened, they all bowed down and shouted, "The LORD is God! The LORD is God!"

Just then, Elijah said, "Grab the prophets of Baal! Don't let any of them get away."

So the people captured the prophets and took them to Kishon River, where Elijah killed every one of them.

Elijah told Ahab, "Get something to eat and drink. I hear a heavy rain coming."

Ahab left, but Elijah climbed back to the top of Mount Carmel. Then he stooped down with his face almost to the ground and said to his servant, "Look toward the sea."

The servant left. And when he came back, he said, "I looked, but I didn't see anything." Elijah told him to look seven more times.

After the seventh time the servant replied, "I see a small cloud coming this way. But it's no bigger than a fist."

Elijah told him, "Tell Ahab to get his chariot ready and start home now. Otherwise, the rain will stop him."

A few minutes later, it got very cloudy and windy, and rain started pouring down. So Elijah wrapped his coat around himself, and the LORD gave him strength to run all the way to Jezreel. Ahab followed him.

But Jezebel, Ahab's queen, wanted Elijah killed for all that he had done. When Elijah heard this, he fled to the desert, to Mount Sinai. He complained to God, and God said that he would appoint a new king and a new prophet for Israel.

The new prophet was Elisha.

### Elijah Is Taken to Heaven

2 Kings
2.11-14

Elijah and Elisha were walking along talking, when suddenly there appeared between them a flaming chariot pulled by fiery horses. Right away, a strong wind took Elijah up into heaven. Elisha saw this and shouted, "Israel's cavalry and chariots have taken my master away!" After Elijah had gone, Elisha tore his clothes in sorrow.

Elijah's coat had fallen off, so Elisha picked it up and walked back to the Jordan River. He struck the water with the coat and wondered, "Will the LORD perform miracles for me as he did for Elijah?" As soon as Elisha did this, a dry path opened up through the water, and he walked across.

# The Prophet Amos

As time went on, the kings and people of Israel were not loyal to the LORD their God. Yet they offered sacrifices to him and held festivals in his honor. At the same time, many of them offered sacrifices to idols. They did not live as God's people, they did not obey God and they mistreated each other. They cheated each other in business; they lied to each other and deceived each other. The powerful oppressed the weak and did not keep their promises. The rich desired more riches and did not care for the poor who lived in need and misery.

God sent prophets to warn the people of Israel that the LORD would punish them if they did not turn away from their sins and do what was right in the eyes of the LORD. One of these prophets was Amos. He received words from God which he then spoke to the Israelites:

## *The LORD Judges the People of Israel*

Amos
5.10-15

You people hate judges and honest witnesses;
    you abuse the poor and demand heavy taxes from them.
You have built expensive homes, but you won't enjoy them;
    you have planted vineyards, but you will get no wine.
I am the LORD, and I know your terrible sins.
You cheat honest people and take bribes;
    you rob the poor of justice.
Times are so evil that anyone with good sense
    will keep quiet.

If you really want to live, you must stop doing wrong
    and start doing right.
I, the LORD God All-Powerful, will then be on your side,
    just as you claim I am.

Choose good instead of evil! See that justice is done.
Maybe I, the LORD All-Powerful,
      will be kind to what's left of your people.

Amos
5.21-25

I, the LORD, hate and despise your religious celebrations
      and your times of worship.
I won't accept your offerings or animal sacrifices—
      not even your very best.
No more of your noisy songs!
      I won't listen when you play your harps.
But let justice and fairness flow like a river
      that never runs dry.

Israel, for forty years you wandered in the desert,
      without bringing offerings or sacrifices to me.

Amos
5.27

I will force you to march as captives beyond Damascus.
      I, the LORD God All-Powerful, have spoken!

## The LORD Will Punish the People of Israel

Amos
8.4-12

You people crush those in need and wipe out the poor.
You say to yourselves, "How much longer before the end
of the New Moon Festival?
When will the Sabbath be over?
Our wheat is ready, and we want to sell it now.
We can't wait to cheat
and charge high prices for the grain we sell.
We will use dishonest scales and mix dust in the grain.
Those who are needy and poor don't have any money.
We will make them our slaves
for the price of a pair of sandals."

I, the LORD, won't forget any of this,
though you take great pride in your ancestor Jacob.
Your country will tremble, and you will mourn.
It will be like the Nile Rive that rises and overflows,
then sinks back down.

138

On that day, I, the LORD God,
will make the sun go down at noon,
   and I will turn daylight into darkness.
Your festivals and joyful singing will turn into sorrow.
You will wear sackcloth and shave your heads,
   as you would at the death of your only son.
It will be a horrible day.

I, the LORD, also promise you a terrible shortage,
   but not of food and water.
You will hunger and thirst to hear my message.
You will search everywhere—
   from north to south, from east to west.
You will go all over the earth,
seeking a message from me, the LORD.
   But you won't find one.

# Israel's Downfall

## An Assyrian King Captures Israel

The Israelites did not listen to Amos or to the other prophets. Therefore the punishment had to come. Hoshea was then king in Israel.

2 Kings 17.3-8

During Hoshea's rule, King Shalmaneser of Assyria invaded Israel; he took control of the country and made Hoshea pay taxes. But later, Hoshea refused to pay the taxes and asked King So of Egypt to help him rebel. When Shalmaneser found out, he arrested Hoshea and put him in prison.

Shalmaneser invaded Israel and attacked the city of Samaria for three years, before capturing it in the ninth year of Hoshea's rule. The Assyrian king took the Israelites away to Assyria as prisoners. He forced some of them to live in the town of Halah, others to live near the Habor River in the territory of Gozan, and still others to live in towns where the Median people lived.

All of this happened because the people of Israel had sinned against the LORD their God, who had rescued them from Egypt, where they had been slaves. They worshiped foreign gods, followed the customs of the nations that the LORD had forced out of Israel, and were just as sinful as the Israelite kings.

## The Prophet Isaiah

God sent prophets to Judah also. One of them was Isaiah. He pointed out what the evil people were doing. For that, he lost his friends and he was often persecuted. But he remained obedient to the LORD.

## God Calls Isaiah

Isaiah
6.1-12

In the year that King Uzziah died, I had a vision of the LORD. He was on his throne high above, and his robe filled the temple. Flaming creatures with six wings each were flying over him. They covered their faces with two of their wings and their bodies with two more. They used the other two wings for flying, as they shouted,

"Holy, holy, holy, LORD All-Powerful!
The earth is filled with your glory."

As they shouted, the doorposts of the temple shook, and the temple was filled with smoke. Then I cried out, "I'm doomed! Everything I say is sinful, and so are the words of everyone around me. Yet I have seen the King, the LORD All-Powerful."

One of the flaming creatures flew over to me with a burning coal that it had taken from the altar with a pair of metal tongs. It touched my lips with the hot coal and said, "This has touched your lips. Your sins are forgiven, and you are no longer guilty."

After this, I heard the LORD ask, "Is there anyone I can send? Will someone go for us?"

"I'll go," I answered. "Send me!"

Then the LORD told me to go and speak this message to the people:

"You will listen and listen, but never understand.
You will look and look, but never see."

The LORD also said,

"Make these people stubborn!
Make them stop up their ears,
cover their eyes, and fail to understand.
Don't let them turn to me and be healed."

Then I asked the LORD, "How long will this last?"

The LORD answered:

   Until their towns are destroyed and their houses are deserted, until their fields are empty, and I have sent them far away, leaving their land in ruins.

Isaiah prophesied about the judgment and punishment due to the people because they had forsaken God. But he also prophesied that a time would come when God would make peace among people. God would at that time send the great Prince of Peace.

## Future Peace without War

Isaiah
2.1-5

This is the message that I was given about Judah and Jerusalem:
> In the future, the mountain with the LORD's temple
> > will be the highest of all.
> It will reach above the hills; every nation will rush to it.
> Many people will come and say,
> "Let's go to the mountain of the LORD God of Jacob
> > and worship in his temple."

> The LORD will teach us his Law from Jerusalem,
> > and we will obey him.
> He will settle arguments between nations.
> They will pound their swords and their spears
> > into rakes and shovels;
> they will never make war or attack one another.
> > People of Israel, let's live by the light of the LORD.

## The Birth of the Son of David

Isaiah
9.1-6

But those who have suffered will no longer be in pain. The territories of Zebulun and Naphtali in Galilee were once hated. But this land of the Gentiles across the Jordan River and along the Mediterranean Sea will be greatly respected.
> Those who walked in the dark have seen a bright light.
> And it shines upon everyone who lives in the land
> > of darkest shadows.
> Our LORD, you have made your nation stronger.
> Because of you, its people are glad and celebrate
> > like workers at harvest time
> > or like soldiers dividing up what they have taken.

You have broken the power of those who abused
    and enslaved your people.
You have rescued them just as you saved your people
    from Midian.
The boots of marching warriors
    and the blood-stained uniforms have been fed to flames
    and eaten by fire.

A child has been born for us. We have been given a son
    who will be our ruler.
His names will be Wonderful Advisor and Mighty God,
    Eternal Father and Prince of Peace.

## *The Son of David and the Peaceful Kingdom*

Isaiah
11.1-10

Like a branch that sprouts from a stump,
    someone from David's family will someday be king.
The Spirit of the LORD will be with him
    to give him understanding, wisdom, and insight.
He will be powerful, and he will know
    and honor the LORD.
His greatest joy will be to obey the LORD.

This king won't judge by appearances or listen to rumors.
The poor and the needy will be treated with fairness
    and with justice.
His word will be law everywhere in the land,
    and criminals will be put to death.
Honesty and fairness will be his royal robes.

Leopards will lie down with young goats,
    and wolves will rest with lambs.
Calves and lions will eat together
    and be cared for by little children.
Cows and bears will share the same pasture;
their young will rest side by side.
    Lions and oxen will both eat straw.

Little children will play near snake holes.
They will stick their hands into dens of poisonous snakes
   and never be hurt.

Nothing harmful will take place
   on the LORD's holy mountain.
Just as water fills the sea,
the land will be filled with people
   who know and honor the LORD.
The time is coming when one of David's descendants will be the signal for the people of all nations to come together. They will follow his advice, and his own nation will become famous.

# Judah's Downfall

## The Babylonian King Captures Jerusalem

2 Kings
24.10-14

King Nebuchadnezzar of Babylonia sent troops to attack Jerusalem soon after Jehoiachin became king. During the attack, Nebuchadnezzar himself arrived at the city. Jehoiachin immediately surrendered, together with his mother and his servants, as well as his army officers and officials. Then Nebuchadnezzar had Jehoiachin arrested. These things took place in the eighth year of Nebuchadnezzar's rule in Babylonia.

The LORD had warned that someday the treasures would be taken from the royal palace and from the temple, including the gold objects that Solomon had made for the temple. And that's exactly what Nebuchadnezzar ordered his soldiers to do. He also led away as prisoners the Jerusalem officials, the military leaders, and the skilled workers—ten thousand in all. Only the very poorest people were left in Judah.

## The Exiled Jews Shall Return

The prophet Jeremiah also returned to Jerusalem. He had repeatedly warned the king and the people that disaster would strike if they would continue in their wicked ways. But they would not listen. After the disaster, and when all but the poorest of the peasants were taken into captivity in Babylonia, Jeremiah prophesied in a letter that the LORD would again lead his people back home.

Jeremiah
29.1,2

I had been left in Jerusalem when King Nebuchadnezzar took many of the people of Jerusalem and Judah to Babylonia as prisoners, including King Jehoiachin, his mother, his officials, and the metal workers and others in Jerusalem who were skilled in making things.

So I wrote a letter to the prophets, the priests, the leaders, and the rest of our people in Babylonia.

Jeremiah
29.3b-7

In the letter, I wrote that the LORD All-Powerful, the God of Israel, had said:

I had you taken from Jerusalem to Babylonia. Now I tell you to settle there and build houses. Plant gardens and eat what you grow in them. Get married and have children, then help your sons find wives and help your daughters find husbands, so they can have children as well. I want your numbers to grow, not to get smaller.

Pray for peace in Babylonia and work hard to make it prosperous. The more successful that nation is, the better off you will be.

Jeremiah
29.10-14

After Babylonia has been the strongest nation for seventy years, I will be kind and bring you back to Jerusalem, just as I have promised. I will bless you with a future filled with hope—a future of success, not of suffering. You will turn back to me and ask for help, and I will answer your prayers. You will worship me with all your heart, and I will be with you and accept your worship. Then I will gather you from all the nations where I scattered you, and you will return to Jerusalem.

# They Shall Be Comforted

Isaiah also prophesied concerning God's promises of salvation to the majority of Jews in captivity in Babylon.

Isaiah
40.1-5

Our God has said:
"Encourage my people! Give them comfort.
    Speak kindly to Jerusalem and announce:
Your slavery is past; your punishment is over.
    I, the LORD, made you pay double for your sins."

Someone is shouting:
"Clear a path in the desert! Make a straight road
    for the LORD our God.
Fill in the valleys; flatten every hill and mountain.
    Level the rough and rugged ground.
Then the glory of the LORD will appear for all to see.
    The LORD has promised this!"

## *The LORD's Suffering Servant Who Is To Come*

Isaiah
53.4-9

He suffered and endured great pain for us,
    but we thought his suffering was punishment from God.
He was wounded and crushed because of our sins;
    by taking our punishment, he made us completely well.
All of us were like sheep that had wandered off.
We had each gone our own way,
    but the LORD gave him the punishment we deserved.

He was painfully abused, but he did not complain.
He was silent like a lamb being led to the butcher,
    as quiet as a sheep having its wool cut off.

He was condemned to death without a fair trial.
    Who could have imagined what would happen to him?
His life was taken away because of the sinful things
    my people had done.
He wasn't dishonest or violent,
    but he was buried in a tomb of cruel and rich people.

## *God's Mercy and God's Word*

Isaiah
55.6-11

Turn to the LORD! He can still be found.
    Call out to God! He is near.
Give up your crooked ways and your evil thoughts.
Return to the LORD our God.
    He will be merciful and forgive your sins.

The LORD says: "My thoughts and my ways
    are not like yours.
Just as the heavens are higher than the earth,
    my thoughts and my ways are higher than yours.

"Rain and snow fall from the sky.
But they don't return without watering the earth
that produces seeds to plant and grain to eat.
That's how it is with my words.
They don't return to me without doing everything
I send them to do."

# Daniel

## *Daniel and His Friends in the Court of the King of Babylon*

One of the Jewish captives who was taken to Babylon by King Nebuchadnezzar was a young man called Daniel.

Daniel
1.3-7

One day the king ordered Ashpenaz, his highest palace official, to choose some young men from the royal family of Judah and from other leading Jewish families. The king said, "They must be healthy, handsome, smart, wise, educated, and fit to serve in the royal palace. Teach them how to speak and write our language and give them the same food and wine that I am served. Train them for three years, and then they can become court officials."

Four of the young Jews chosen were Daniel, Hananiah, Mishael, and Azariah, all from the tribe of Judah. But the king's chief official gave them Babylonian names: Daniel became Belteshazzar, Hananiah became Shadrach, Mishael became Meshach, and Azariah became Abednego.

Daniel
1.17

God made the four young men smart and wise. They read a lot of books and became well educated. Daniel could also tell the meaning of dreams and visions.

Daniel
3.1

King Nebuchadnezzar ordered a gold statue to be built ninety feet high and nine feet wide. He had it set up in Dura Valley near the city of Babylon.

Daniel
3.4-30

Then an official stood up and announced:

People of every nation and race, now listen to the king's command! Trumpets, flutes, harps, and all other kinds of musical instruments will soon start playing. When you hear the music, you must bow down and worship the statue that King Nebuchadnezzar has set up. Anyone who refuses will at once be thrown into a flaming furnace.

As soon as the people heard the music, they bowed down and worshiped the gold statue that the king had set up.

Some Babylonians used this as a chance to accuse the Jews to King Nebuchadnezzar. They said, "Your Majesty, we hope you live forever! You commanded everyone to bow down and worship the gold statue when the music played. And you said that anyone who did not bow down and worship it would be thrown into a flaming furnace. Sir, you appointed three men to high positions in Babylon Province, but they have disobeyed you. Those Jews, Shadrach, Meshach, and Abednego, refuse to worship your gods and the statue you have set up."

King Nebuchadnezzar was furious. So he sent for the three young men and said, "I hear that you refuse to worship my gods and the gold statue I have set up. Now I am going to give you one more chance. If you bow down and worship the statue when you hear the music, everything will be all right. But if you don't, you will at once be thrown into a flaming furnace. No god can save you from me."

The three men replied, "Your Majesty, we don't need to defend ourselves. The God we worship can save us from you and your flaming furnace. But even if he doesn't, we still won't worship your gods and the gold statue you have set up."

Nebuchadnezzar's face twisted with anger at the three men. And he ordered the furnace to be heated seven times hotter than usual. Next, he commanded some of his strongest soldiers to tie up the men and throw them into the flaming furnace. The king wanted it done at that very moment. So the soldiers tied up Shadrach, Meshach, and Abednego and threw them into the flaming furnace with all of their clothes still on, including their turbans. The fire was so hot that flames leaped out and killed the soldiers.

Suddenly the king jumped up and shouted, "Weren't only three men tied up and thrown into the fire?"

"Yes, Your Majesty," the people answered.

"But I see four men walking around in the fire," the king replied. "None of them is tied up or harmed, and the fourth one looks like a god."

Nebuchadnezzar went closer to the flaming furnace and said to the three young men, "You servants of the Most High God, come out at once!"

They came out, and the king's high officials, governors, and advisors all crowded around them. The men were not burned, their hair wasn't scorched, and their clothes didn't even smell like smoke. King Nebuchadnezzar said:

Praise their God for sending an angel to rescue his servants! They trusted their God and refused to obey my commands. Yes, they chose to die rather than to worship or serve any god except their own. And I won't allow people of any nation or race to say anything against their God. Anyone who does will be chopped up and their houses will be torn down, because no other god has such great power to save.

After this happened, the king appointed Shadrach, Meshach, and Abednego to even higher positions in Babylon Province.

## Daniel in the Pit of Lions

Belshazzar succeeded his father Nebuchadnezzar as king, but one night he was killed and Darius took over the kingdom.

Daniel
6.2-28

In order to make sure that his government was run properly, Darius put three other officials in charge of the governors. One of these officials was Daniel. And he did his work so much better than the other governors and officials that the king decided to let him govern the whole kingdom.

The other men tried to find something wrong with the way Daniel did his work for the king. But they could not accuse him of anything wrong, because he was honest and faithful and did everything he was supposed to do. Finally, they said to one another, "We will never be able to bring any charge against Daniel, unless it has to do with his religion."

They all went to the king and said:

Your Majesty, we hope you live forever! All of your officials, leaders, advisors, and governors agree that you should make a law forbidding anyone to pray to any god or human except you for the next thirty days. Everyone who disobeys this law must be thrown into a pit of lions. Order this to be written and then sign it, so it cannot be changed, just as no written law of the Medes and Persians can be changed."

So King Darius made the law and had it written down.

Daniel heard about the law, but when he returned home, he went upstairs and prayed in front of the window that faced Jerusalem. In the same way that he had always done, he knelt down in prayer three times a day, giving thanks to God.

The men who had spoken to the king watched Daniel and saw him praying to his God for help. They went back to the king and said, "Didn't you make a law that forbids anyone to pray to any god or human except you for the next thirty days? And doesn't the law say that everyone who disobeys it will be thrown into a pit of lions?"

"Yes, that's the law I made," the king agreed. "And just like all written laws of the Medes and Persians, it cannot be changed."

The men then told the king, "That Jew named Daniel, who was brought here as a captive, refuses to obey you or the law that you ordered to be written. And he still prays to his god three times a day." The king was really upset to hear about this, and for the rest of the day he tried to think how he could save Daniel.

At sunset the men returned and said, "Your Majesty, remember that no written law of the Medes and Persians can be changed, not even by the king."

So Darius ordered Daniel to be brought out and thrown into a pit of lions. But he said to Daniel, "You have been faithful to your God, and I pray that he will rescue you."

A stone was rolled over the pit, and it was sealed. Then Darius and his officials stamped the seal to show that no one should let Daniel out. All night long the king could not sleep. He did not eat anything, and he would not let anyone come in to entertain him.

At daybreak the king got up and ran to the pit. He was anxious and shouted, "Daniel, you were faithful and served your God. Was he able to save you from the lions?"

Daniel answered, "Your Majesty, I hope you live forever! My God knew that I was innocent, and he sent an angel to keep the lions from eating me. Your Majesty, I have never done anything to hurt you."

The king was relieved to hear Daniel's voice, and he gave orders for him to be taken out of the pit. Daniel's faith in his God had kept him from being harmed. And the king ordered the men who had brought charges against Daniel to be thrown into the pit, together with their wives and children. But before they even reached the bottom, the lions ripped them to pieces.

King Darius then sent this message to all people of every nation and race in the world:
"Greetings to all of you!
I command everyone in my kingdom
    to worship and honor the God of Daniel.
He is the living God, the one who lives forever.
    His power and his kingdom will never end.

He rescues people and sets them free
　　by working great miracles.
Daniel's God has rescued him
　　from the power of the lions."
　　All went well for Daniel while Darius was king, and even when
Cyrus the Persian ruled.

# A Group of Jewish Exiles Returns from Babylon

## *The Return Home*

Ezra

1.1-11

Years ago the LORD sent Jeremiah with a message about a promise for the people of Israel. Then in the first year that Cyrus was king of Persia, the LORD kept his promise by having Cyrus send this official message to all parts of his kingdom:

I am King Cyrus of Persia.

The LORD God of heaven, who is also the God of Israel, has made me the ruler of all nations on earth. And he has chosen me to build a temple for him in Jerusalem, which is in Judah. The LORD God will watch over and encourage any of his people who want to go back to Jerusalem and help build the temple.

Everyone else must provide what is needed. They must give money, supplies, and animals, as well as gifts for rebuilding God's temple.

Many people felt that the LORD God wanted them to help rebuild his temple, and they made plans to go to Jerusalem. Among them were priests, Levites, and leaders of the tribes of Judah and Benjamin. The others helped by giving silver articles, gold, personal possessions, cattle, and other valuable gifts, as well as offerings for the temple.

King Cyrus gave back the things that Nebuchadnezzar had taken from the LORD's temple in Jerusalem and had put in the temple of his own gods. Cyrus placed Mithredath, his chief treasurer, in charge of these things. Mithredath counted them and gave a list to Sheshbazzar, the governor of Judah. Included among them were: 30 large gold dishes; 1,000 large silver dishes; 29 other dishes; 30 gold bowls; 410 silver bowls; and 1,000 other articles.

Altogether, there were 5,400 gold and silver dishes, bowls, and other articles. Sheshbazzar took them with him when he and the others returned to Jerusalem from Babylonia.

## Rebuilding the Temple

Ezra
3.8

During the second month of the second year after the people had returned from Babylonia, they started rebuilding the LORD's temple. Zerubbabel son of Shealtiel, Joshua son of Jozadak, the priests, the Levites, and everyone else who had returned started working. Every Levite over twenty years of age was put in charge of some part of the work.

Ezra
3.10-13

When the builders had finished laying the foundation of the temple, the priests put on their robes and blew trumpets in honor of the LORD, while the Levites from the family of Asaph praised God with cymbals. All of them followed the instructions given years before by King David. They praised the LORD and gave thanks as they took turns singing:

"The LORD is good!
His faithful love for Israel
   will last forever."

Everyone started shouting and praising the LORD because work on the foundation of the temple had begun. Many of the older priests and Levites and the heads of families cried aloud because they remembered seeing the first temple years before. But others were so happy that they celebrated with joyful shouts. Their shouting and crying were so noisy that it all sounded alike and could be heard a long way off.

Ezra
6.16

The people of Israel, the priests, the Levites, and everyone else who had returned from exile were happy and celebrated as they dedicated God's temple.

# Jonah

## *Jonah Flees*

One day the LORD told Jonah, the son of Amittai, to go to the great city of Nineveh and say to the people, "The LORD has seen your terrible sins. You are doomed!"

Instead, Jonah ran from the LORD. He went to the seaport of Joppa and bought a ticket on a ship that was going to Spain. Then he got on the ship and sailed away to escape.

But the LORD made a strong wind blow, and such a bad storm came up that the ship was about to be broken to pieces. The sailors were frightened, and they all started praying to their gods. They even threw the ship's cargo overboard to make the ship lighter.

All this time, Jonah was down below deck, sound asleep. The ship's captain went to him and said, "How can you sleep at a time like this? Get up and pray to your God! Maybe he will have pity on us and keep us from drowning."

Finally, the sailors got together and said, "Let's ask our gods to show us who caused all this trouble." It turned out to be Jonah.

They started asking him, "Are you the one who brought all this trouble on us? What business are you in? Where do you come from? What is your country? Who are your people?"

Jonah answered, "I'm a Hebrew, and I worship the LORD God of heaven, who made the sea and the dry land."

When the sailors heard this, they were frightened, because Jonah had already told them he was running from the LORD. Then they said, "Do you know what you have done?"

The storm kept getting worse, until finally the sailors asked him, "What should we do with you to make the sea calm down?"

Jonah told them, "Throw me into the sea, and it will calm down. I'm the cause of this terrible storm."

The sailors tried their best to row to the shore. But they could not do it, and the storm kept getting worse every minute. So they prayed to the LORD, "Please don't let us drown for taking this man's life. Don't hold us guilty for killing an innocent man. All of this happened because you wanted it to." Then they threw Jonah overboard, and the sea calmed down. The sailors were so terrified that they offered a sacrifice to the LORD and made all kinds of promises.

The LORD sent a big fish to swallow Jonah, and Jonah was inside the fish for three days and three nights.

## *Jonah in the Belly of a Fish*

Jonah
2. 1-10

From inside the fish, Jonah prayed to the LORD his God:
> When I was in trouble, LORD, I prayed to you,
>> and you listened to me.
> From deep in the world of the dead,
>> I begged for your help, and you answered my prayer.
>
> You threw me down to the bottom of the sea.
> The water was churning all around;
>> I was completely covered by your mighty waves.
> I thought I was swept away from your sight,
>> never again to see your holy temple.
>
> I was almost drowned by the swirling waters
>> that surrounded me.
> Seaweed had wrapped around my head.
> I had sunk down below the underwater mountains;
>> I knew that forever, I would be a prisoner there.
>
> But, you, LORD God, rescued me from that pit.
> When my life was slipping away, I remembered you—
>> and in your holy temple you heard my prayer.

All who worship worthless idols
    turn from the God who offers them mercy.
But with shouts of praise, I will offer a sacrifice
    to you, my LORD.
I will keep my promise, because you are the one
    with power to save.

The LORD commanded the fish to vomit up Jonah on the shore. And it did.

## *Jonah in Nineveh*

Jonah
3.1-10

Once again the LORD told Jonah to go to that great city of Nineveh and preach his message of doom.

Jonah obeyed the LORD and went to Nineveh. The city was so big that it took three days just to walk through it. After walking for a day, Jonah warned the people, "Forty days from now, Nineveh will be destroyed!"

They believed God's message and set a time when they would go without eating to show their sorrow. Then everyone in the city, no matter who they were, dressed in sackcloth.

When the king of Nineveh heard what was happening, he also dressed in sackcloth; he left the royal palace and sat in dust. Then he and his officials sent out an order for everyone in the city to obey. It said:

None of you or your animals may eat or drink a thing. Each of you must wear sackcloth, and you must even put sackcloth on your animals.

You must also pray to the LORD God with all your heart and stop being sinful and cruel. Maybe God will change his mind and have mercy on us, so we won't be destroyed.

When God saw that the people had stopped doing evil things, he had pity and did not destroy them as he had planned.

## Jonah's Anger

Jonah

4.1-11

Jonah was really upset and angry. So he prayed:

Our LORD, I knew from the very beginning that you wouldn't destroy Nineveh. That's why I left my own country and headed for Spain. You are a kind and merciful God, and you are very patient. You always show love, and you don't like to punish anyone, not even foreigners.

Now let me die! I'd be better off dead.

The LORD replied, "What right do you have to be angry?"

Jonah then left through the east gate of the city and made a shelter to protect himself from the sun. He sat under the shelter, waiting to see what would happen to Nineveh.

The LORD made a vine grow up to shade Jonah's head and protect him from the sun. Jonah was very happy to have the vine, but early the next morning the LORD sent a worm to chew on the vine, and the vine dried up. During the day the LORD sent a scorching wind, and the sun beat down on Jonah's head, making him feel faint. Jonah was ready to die, and he shouted, "I wish I were dead!"

But the LORD asked, "Jonah, do you have the right to be angry about the vine?"

"Yes, I do," he answered, "and I'm angry enough to die."

But the LORD said:

You are concerned about a vine that you did not plant or take care of, a vine that grew up in one night and died the next. In that city of Nineveh there are more than a hundred twenty thousand people who cannot tell right from wrong, and many cattle are also there. Don't you think I should be concerned about that big city?

# From the Book of Psalms

## *The Wonderful Name of the LORD*

Psalm
8.1-9

Our LORD and Ruler,
   your name is wonderful everywhere on earth!
You let your glory be seen in the heavens above.
With praises from children and from tiny infants,
   you have built a fortress.
It makes your enemies silent,
   and all who turn against you are left speechless.

I often think of the heavens your hands have made,
   and of the moon and stars you put in place.
Then I ask, "Why do you care about us humans?
   Why are you concerned for us weaklings?"
You made us a little lower than you yourself,
   and you have crowned us with glory and honor.

You let us rule everything your hands have made.
And you put all of it under our power—
   the sheep and the cattle, and every wild animal,
   the birds in the sky, the fish in the sea,
   and all ocean creatures.

Our LORD and Ruler,
   your name is wonderful everywhere on earth!

# The Good Shepherd

Psalm
23.1-6

You, LORD, are my shepherd. I will never be in need.
    You let me rest in fields of green grass.
You lead me to streams of peaceful water,
    and you refresh my life.

You are true to your name,
    and you lead me along the right paths.
I may walk through valleys as dark as death,
    but I won't be afraid.
You are with me,
    and your shepherd's rod makes me feel safe.

You treat me to a feast, while my enemies watch.
You honor me as your guest,
    and you fill my cup until it overflows.
Your kindness and love will always be with me
each day of my life,
    and I will live forever in your house, LORD.

# A Prayer for Forgiveness

Psalm
51.3-6

I know about my sins,
    and I cannot forget my terrible guilt.
You are really the one I have sinned against;
    I have disobeyed you and have done wrong.
So it is right and fair for you
    to correct and punish me.

I have sinned and done wrong since the day I was born.
But you want complete honesty,
    so teach me true wisdom.

Psalm
51.11-14

Don't chase me away from you
    or take your Holy Spirit away from me.

169

Make me as happy as you did when you saved me;
    make me want to obey!
I will teach sinners your Law,
    and they will return to you.
Keep me from any deadly sin. Only you can save me!
    Then I will shout and sing about your power to save.


## The LORD Is Always Near

Psalm
139.1-18

You have looked deep into my heart, LORD,
    and you know all about me.
You know when I am resting or when I am working,
    and from heaven you discover my thoughts.

You notice everything I do and everywhere I go.
Before I even speak a word,
    you know what I will say,
and with your powerful arm
    you protect me from every side.
I can't understand all of this!
    Such wonderful knowledge is far above me.

Where could I go to escape
    from your Spirit or from your sight?
If I were to climb up to the highest heavens,
    you would be there.
If I were to dig down to the world of the dead
    you would also be there.

Suppose I had wings like the dawning day
    and flew across the ocean.
Even then your powerful arm
    would guide and protect me.
Or suppose I said, "I'll hide in the dark
    until night comes to cover me over."

But you see in the dark
    because daylight and dark are all the same to you.

You are the one who put me together
    inside my mother's body,
and I praise you
    because of the wonderful way you created me.
Everything you do is marvelous!
    Of this I have no doubt.

Nothing about me is hidden from you!
I was secretly woven together
    deep in the earth below,
but with your own eyes
    you saw my body being formed.
Even before I was born, you had written in your book
    everything I would do.

Your thoughts are far beyond my understanding,
    much more than I could ever imagine.
I try to count your thoughts,
    but they outnumber the grains of sand on the beach.
And when I awake, I will find you nearby.

Psalm
139.23,24

Look deep into my heart, God,
    and find out everything I am thinking.
Don't let me follow evil ways,
    but lead me in the way that time has proven true.

# From the Song of Songs

## *I Love Him*

Song of Songs
2.1-17

*She Speaks:*
>  I am merely a rose from the land of Sharon,
>> a lily from the valley.

*He Speaks:*
>  My darling, when compared with other young women,
>> you are a lily among thorns.

*She Speaks:*
>  And you, my love, are an apple tree
>> among trees of the forest.
>  Your shade brought me pleasure;
>> your fruit was sweet.
>  You led me to your banquet room
>> and showered me with love.
>  Refresh and strengthen me with raisins and apples.
>> I am hungry for love!
>  Put your left hand under my head
>> and embrace me with your right arm.

>  Young women of Jerusalem,
>  promise me by the power of deer and gazelles
>> never to awaken love before it is ready.

*She Speaks:*
　　I hear the voice of the one I love,
　　as he comes leaping over mountains and hills
　　　　like a deer or a gazelle.
　　Now he stands outside our wall,
　　　　looking through the window and speaking to me.

*He Speaks:*
　　My darling, I love you! Let's go away together.
　　Winter is past, the rain has stopped;
　　　　flowers cover the earth, it's time to sing.
　　　　The cooing of doves is heard in our land.
　　Fig trees are bearing fruit,
　　while blossoms on grapevines
　　　　fill the air with perfume.
　　My darling, I love you! Let's go away together.
　　You are my dove hiding among the rocks
　　　　on the side of a cliff.
　　Let me see how lovely you are!
　　　　Let me hear the sound of your melodious voice.
　　Our vineyards are in blossom;
　　we must catch the little foxes
　　　　that destroy the vineyards.

*She Speaks:*
　　My darling, I am yours, and you are mine,
　　　　as you feed your sheep among the lilies.
　　Pretend to be a young deer dancing on mountain slopes
　　　　until daylight comes and shadows fade away.

Song of Songs
3.1-5
While in bed at night, I reached for the one I love
with heart and soul.
　　I looked for him, but he wasn't there.
So I searched through the town for the one I love.
　　I looked on every street, but he wasn't there.
I even asked the guards patrolling the town,
　　"Have you seen the one I love so much?"
Right after that, I found him. I held him

and would not let go until I had taken him
    to the home of my mother.
Young women of Jerusalem,
promise me by the power of deer and gazelles,
    never to awaken love before it is ready.

# From the Book of Ecclesiastes

## *Everything Has Its Time*

Ecclesiastes
3.1-17

Everything on earth has its own time and its own season.
There is a time for birth and death, planting and reaping,
    for killing and healing, destroying and building,
    for crying and laughing, weeping and dancing,
    for throwing stones and gathering stones,
    embracing and parting.
There is a time for finding and losing, keeping and giving,
    for tearing and sewing, listening and speaking.
There is also a time for love and hate, for war and peace.

What do we gain by all of our hard work? I have seen what difficult things God demands of us. God makes everything happen at the right time. Yet none of us can ever fully understand all he has done, and he puts questions in our minds about the past and the future. I know the best thing we can do is to always enjoy life, because God's gift to us is the happiness we get from our food and drink and from the work we do. Everything God has done will last forever; nothing he does can ever be changed. God has done all this, so that we will worship him.

Everything that happens has happened before,
and all that will be has already been—
    God does everything over and over again.

Everywhere on earth I saw violence and injustice instead of fairness and justice. So I told myself that God has set a time and a place for everything. He will judge everyone, both the wicked and the good.

# New Testament

# Jesus' Childhood

## *John's Birth Announced*

Luke
1.5-16

When Herod was king of Judea, there was a priest by the name of Zechariah from the priestly group of Abijah. His wife Elizabeth was from the family of Aaron. Both of them were good people and pleased the Lord God by obeying all that he had commanded. But they did not have children. Elizabeth could not have any, and both Zechariah and Elizabeth were already old.

One day Zechariah's group of priests were on duty, and he was serving God as a priest. According to the custom of the priests, he had been chosen to go into the Lord's temple that day and to burn incense, while the people stood outside praying.

All at once an angel from the Lord appeared to Zechariah at the right side of the altar. Zechariah was confused and afraid when he saw the angel. But the angel told him:

Don't be afraid, Zechariah! God has heard your prayers. Your wife Elizabeth will have a son, and you must name him John. His birth will make you very happy, and many people will be glad. Your son will be a great servant of the Lord. He must never drink wine or beer, and the power of the Holy Spirit will be with him from the time he is born.

John will lead many people in Israel to turn back to the Lord their God.

Luke
1.18-25

Zechariah said to the angel, "How will I know this is going to happen? My wife and I are both very old."

The angel answered, "I am Gabriel, God's servant, and I was sent to tell you this good news. You have not believed what I have said. So you will not be able to say a thing until all this happens. But everything will take place when it is supposed to."

The crowd was waiting for Zechariah and kept wondering why he was staying so long in the temple. When he did come out, he could not speak, and they knew he had seen a vision. He motioned to them with his hands, but did not say a thing.

When Zechariah's time of service in the temple was over, he went home. Soon after that, his wife was expecting a baby, and for five months she did not leave the house. She said to herself, "What the Lord has done for me will keep people from looking down on me."

## An Angel Visits Mary

Luke
1.26-38

One month later God sent the angel Gabriel to the town of Nazareth in Galilee with a message for a virgin named Mary. She was engaged to Joseph from the family of King David. The angel greeted Mary and said, "You are truly blessed! The Lord is with you."

Mary was confused by the angel's words and wondered what they meant. Then the angel told Mary, "Don't be afraid! God is pleased with you, and you will have a son. His name will be Jesus. He will be great and will be called the Son of God Most High. The Lord God will make him king, as his ancestor David was. He will rule the people of Israel forever, and his kingdom will never end."

Mary asked the angel, "How can this happen? I am not married!"

The angel answered, "The Holy Spirit will come down to you, and God's power will come over you. So your child will be called the holy Son of God. Your relative Elizabeth is also going to have a son, even though she is old. No one thought she could ever have a baby, but in three months she will have a son. Nothing is impossible for God!"

Mary said, "I am the Lord's servant! Let it happen as you have said." And the angel left her.

## Mary Visits Elizabeth

Luke
1.39-42

A short time later Mary hurried to a town in the hill country of Judea. She went into Zechariah's home, where she greeted Elizabeth. When Elizabeth heard Mary's greeting, her baby moved within her.

The Holy Spirit came upon Elizabeth. Then in a loud voice she said to Mary:

God has blessed you more than any other woman! He has also blessed the child you will have.

Luke
1.46,47

Mary said:

With all my heart I praise the Lord,
  and I am glad because of God my Savior.

Luke
1.49,50

God All-Powerful has done great things for me,
  and his name is holy.
He always shows mercy
  to everyone who worships him.

Luke
1.56

Mary stayed with Elizabeth about three months. Then she went back home.

## The Birth of John

Luke
1.57-66

When Elizabeth's son was born, her neighbors and relatives heard how kind the Lord had been to her, and they too were glad.

Eight days later they did for the child what the Law of Moses commands. They were going to name him Zechariah, after his father. But Elizabeth said, "No! His name is John."

The people argued, "No one in your family has ever been named John." So they motioned to Zechariah to find out what he wanted to name his son.

Zechariah asked for a writing tablet. Then he wrote, "His name is John." Everyone was amazed. Right away, Zechariah started speaking and praising God.

All the neighbors were frightened because of what had happened, and everywhere in the hill country people kept talking about these things. Everyone who heard about this wondered what this child would grow up to be. They knew that the Lord was with him.

As John grew up, God's Spirit gave him great power. John lived in the desert until the time he was sent to the people of Israel.

## *The Birth of Jesus*

About that time Emperor Augustus gave orders for the names of all the people to be listed in record books. These first records were made when Quirinius was governor of Syria.

Everyone had to go to their own hometown to be listed. So Joseph had to leave Nazareth in Galilee and go to Bethlehem in Judea. Long ago Bethlehem had been King David's hometown, and Joseph went there because he was from David's family.

Mary was engaged to Joseph and traveled with him to Bethlehem. She was soon going to have a baby, and while they were there, she gave birth to her first-born son. She dressed him in baby clothes and laid him on a bed of hay, because there was no room for them in the inn.

That night in the fields near Bethlehem some shepherds were guarding their sheep. All at once an angel came down to them from the Lord, and the brightness of the Lord's glory flashed around them. The shepherds were frightened. But the angel said, "Don't be afraid! I have good news for you, which will make everyone happy. This very day in King David's hometown a Savior was born for you. He is Christ the Lord. You will know who he is, because you will find him dressed in baby clothes and lying on a bed of hay."

Suddenly many other angels came down from heaven and joined in praising God. They said:

"Praise God in heaven!

Peace on earth to everyone who pleases God."

After the angels had left and gone back to heaven, the shepherds said to each other, "Let's go to Bethlehem and see what the Lord has told us about." They hurried off and found Mary and Joseph, and they saw the baby lying on a bed of hay.

When the shepherds saw Jesus, they told his parents what the angel had said about him. Everyone listened and was surprised. But Mary kept thinking about all this and wondering what it meant.

As the shepherds returned to their sheep, they were praising God and saying wonderful things about him. Everything they had seen and heard was just as the angel had said.

## The Wise Men from the East

Matthew

2.1-12

When Jesus was born in the village of Bethlehem in Judea, Herod was king. During this time some wise men from the east came to Jerusalem and said, "Where is the child born to be king of the Jews? We saw his star in the east and have come to worship him."

When King Herod heard about this, he was worried, and so was everyone else in Jerusalem. Herod brought together the chief priests and the teachers of the Law of Moses and asked them, "Where will the Messiah be born?"

They told him, "He will be born in Bethlehem, just as the prophet wrote,

'Bethlehem in the land of Judea,
    you are very important among the towns of Judea.
From your town will come a leader,
    who will be like a shepherd for my people Israel.' "

Herod secretly called in the wise men and asked them when they had first seen the star. He told them, "Go to Bethlehem and search carefully for the child. As soon as you find him, let me know. I want to go and worship him too."

The wise men listened to what the king said and then left. And the star they had seen in the east went on ahead of them until it stopped over the place where the child was. They were thrilled and excited to see the star.

When the men went into the house and saw the child with Mary, his mother, they knelt down and worshiped him. They took out their gifts of gold, frankincense, and myrrh and gave them to him. Later they were warned in a dream not to return to Herod, and they went back home by another road.

## *Herod Orders Children To Be Killed*

Matthew
2.13-16

After the wise men had gone, an angel from the Lord appeared to Joseph in a dream and said, "Get up! Hurry and take the child and his mother to Egypt! Stay there until I tell you to return, because Herod is looking for the child and wants to kill him."

That night, Joseph got up and took his wife and the child to Egypt, where they stayed until Herod died. So the Lord's promise came true, just as the prophet had said, "I called my son out of Egypt."

When Herod found out that the wise men from the east had tricked him, he was very angry. He gave orders for his men to kill all the boys who lived in or near Bethlehem and were two years old and younger. This was based on what he had learned from the wise men.

Matthew
2.19-23

After King Herod died, an angel from the Lord appeared in a dream to Joseph while he was still in Egypt. The angel said, "Get up and take the child and his mother back to Israel. The people who wanted to kill him are now dead."

Joseph got up and left with them for Israel. But when he heard that Herod's son Archelaus was now ruler of Judea, he was afraid to go there. Then in a dream he was told to go to Galilee, and they went to live there in the town of Nazareth. So the Lord's promise came true, just as the prophet had said, "He will be called a Nazarene."

## *The Twelve-Year-Old Jesus in the Temple*

Luke
2.41-52

Every year Jesus' parents went to Jerusalem for Passover. And when Jesus was twelve years old, they all went there as usual for the celebration. After Passover his parents left, but they did not know that Jesus had stayed on in the city. They thought he was traveling with some other people, and they went a whole day before they started looking for him. When they could not find him with their relatives and friends, they went back to Jerusalem and started looking for him there.

Three days later they found Jesus sitting in the temple, listening to the teachers and asking them questions. Everyone who heard him was surprised at how much he knew and at the answers he gave.

When his parents found him, they were amazed. His mother said, "Son, why have you done this to us? Your father and I have been very worried, and we have been searching for you!"

Jesus answered, "Why did you have to look for me? Didn't you know that I would be in my Father's house?" But they did not understand what he meant.

Jesus went back to Nazareth with his parents and obeyed them. His mother kept on thinking about all that had happened.

Jesus became wise, and he grew strong. God was pleased with him and so were the people.

# Jesus Starts His Ministry

## *John Baptizes and Jesus Is Baptized*

Luke
3.9-16

John had lived many years in the desert when God spoke to him. So he moved to the region of the Jordan River. Many people came to hear him preach that they should repent and be baptized to receive forgiveness of sins. And to the people who came to be baptized, he said: "An ax is ready to cut the trees down at their roots. Any tree that doesn't produce good fruit will be cut down and thrown into a fire."

The crowds asked John, "What should we do?"

John told them, "If you have two coats, give one to someone who doesn't have any. If you have food, share it with someone else."

When tax collectors came to be baptized, they asked John, "Teacher, what should we do?"

John told them, "Don't make people pay more than they owe."

Some soldiers asked him, "And what about us? What do we have to do?"

John told them, "Don't force people to pay money to make you leave them alone. Be satisfied with your pay."

Everyone became excited and wondered, "Could John be the Messiah?"

John said, "I am just baptizing with water. But someone more powerful is going to come, and I am not good enough even to untie his sandals. He will baptize you with the Holy Spirit and with fire."

Luke
3.21,22

While everyone else was being baptized, Jesus himself was baptized. Then as he prayed, the sky opened up, and the Holy Spirit came down upon him in the form of a dove. A voice from heaven said, "You are my own dear Son, and I am pleased with you."

## The Temptation of Jesus in the Desert

Luke
4.1-13

When Jesus returned from the Jordan River, the power of the Holy Spirit was with him, and the Spirit led him into the desert. For forty days Jesus was tested by the devil, and during that time he went without eating. When it was all over, he was hungry.

The devil said to Jesus, "If you are God's Son, tell this stone to turn into bread."

Jesus answered, "The Scriptures say, 'No one can live only on food.' "

Then the devil led Jesus up to a high place and quickly showed him all the nations on earth. The devil said, "I will give all this power and glory to you. It has been given to me, and I can give it to anyone I want to. Just worship me, and you can have it all."

Jesus answered, "The Scriptures say:
'Worship the Lord your God
    and serve only him!' "

Finally, the devil took Jesus to Jerusalem and had him stand on top of the temple. The devil said, "If you are God's Son, jump off. The Scriptures say:
'God will tell his angels to take care of you.
They will catch you in their arms,
    and you will not hurt your feet on the stones.' "

Jesus answered, "The Scriptures also say, 'Don't try to test the Lord your God!' "

After the devil had finished testing Jesus in every way possible, he left him for a while.

## Jesus in Nazareth

Luke
4.14-21

Jesus returned to Galilee with the power of the Spirit. News about him spread everywhere. He taught in the Jewish meeting places, and everyone praised him.

Jesus went back to Nazareth, where he had been brought up, and as usual he went to the meeting place on the Sabbath. When he stood up to read from the Scriptures, he was given the book of Isaiah the prophet. He opened it and read,

"The Lord's Spirit has come to me,
because he has chosen me
   to tell the good news to the poor.
The Lord has sent me to announce freedom for prisoners,
to give sight to the blind, to free everyone who suffers,
   and to say, 'This is the year the Lord has chosen.' "

Jesus closed the book, then handed it back to the man in charge and sat down. Everyone in the meeting place looked straight at Jesus.

Then Jesus said to them, "What you have just heard me read has come true today."

## The Wedding in Cana

There was a wedding in Cana. Jesus was there with his mother, and his disciples were also invited.

John
2.3-11

When the wine was all gone, Mary said to Jesus, "They don't have any more wine."

Jesus replied, "Mother, my time hasn't yet come! You must not tell me what to do."

Mary then said to the servants, "Do whatever Jesus tells you to do."

At the feast there were six stone water jars that were used by the people for washing themselves in the way that their religion said they must. Each jar held about twenty or thirty gallons. Jesus told the servants to fill them to the top with water. Then after the jars had been filled, he said, "Now take some water and give it to the man in charge of the feast."

The servants did as Jesus told them, and the man in charge drank some of the water that had now turned into wine. He did not know where the wine had come from, but the servants did. He called the bridegroom over and said, "The best wine is always served first. Then after the guests have had plenty, the other wine is served. But you have kept the best until last!"

This was Jesus' first miracle, and he did it in the village of Cana in Galilee. There Jesus showed his glory, and his disciples put their faith in him.

## One Day in Capernaum

Luke
4.31-40

Jesus went to the town of Capernaum in Galilee and taught the people on the Sabbath. His teaching amazed them because he spoke with power. There in the Jewish meeting place was a man with an evil spirit. He yelled out, "Hey, Jesus of Nazareth, what do you want with us? Are you here to get rid of us? I know who you are! You are God's Holy One."

Jesus ordered the evil spirit to be quiet and come out. The demon threw the man to the ground in front of everyone and left without harming him.

They all were amazed and kept saying to each other, "What kind of teaching is this? He has power to order evil spirits out of people!" News about Jesus spread all over that part of the country.

Jesus left the meeting place and went to Simon's home. When Jesus got there, he was told that Simon's mother-in-law was sick with a high fever. So Jesus went over to her and ordered the fever to go away. Right then she was able to get up and serve them a meal.

After the sun had set, people with all kinds of diseases were brought to Jesus. He put his hands on each one of them and healed them.

## Peter Catches Fish

Luke
5.1-11

Jesus was standing on the shore of Lake Gennesaret, teaching the people as they crowded around him to hear God's message. Near the shore he saw two boats left there by some fishermen who had gone to wash their nets. Jesus got into the boat that belonged to Simon and asked him to row it out a little way from the shore. Then Jesus sat down in the boat to teach the crowd.

When Jesus had finished speaking, he told Simon, "Row the boat out into the deep water and let your nets down to catch some fish."

"Master," Simon answered, "we have worked hard all night long and have not caught a thing. But if you tell me to, I will let the nets down." They did it and caught so many fish that their nets began ripping apart. Then they signaled for their partners in the other boat to come and help them. The men came, and together they filled the two boats so full that they both began to sink.

When Simon Peter saw this happen, he knelt down in front of Jesus and said, "Lord, don't come near me! I am a sinner." Peter and everyone with him were completely surprised at all the fish they had caught. His partners James and John, the sons of Zebedee, were surprised too.

Jesus told Simon, "Don't be afraid! From now on you will bring in people instead of fish." The men pulled their boats up on the shore. Then they left everything and went with Jesus.

## *Jesus Teaches and Heals*

Matthew
4.23-25

Jesus went all over Galilee, teaching in the Jewish meeting places and preaching the good news about God's kingdom. He also healed every kind of disease and sickness. News about him spread all over Syria, and people with every kind of sickness or disease were brought to him. Some of them had a lot of demons in them, others were thought to be crazy, and still others could not walk. But Jesus healed them all.

Large crowds followed Jesus from Galilee and the region around the ten cities known as Decapolis. They also came from Jerusalem, Judea, and from across the Jordan River.

194

# From the Sermon on the Mount

## *God's Kingdom Is at Hand*

Matthew

5.1-12

When Jesus saw the crowds, he went up on the side of a mountain and sat down.

Jesus' disciples gathered around him, and he taught them:
God blesses those people who depend only on him.
They belong to the kingdom of heaven!
God blesses those people who grieve.
They will find comfort!
God blesses those people who are humble.
The earth will belong to them!
God blesses those people who want to obey him
more than to eat or drink.
They will be given what they want!
God blesses those people who are merciful.
They will be treated with mercy!
God blesses those people whose hearts are pure.
They will see him!
God blesses those people who make peace.
They will be called his children!
God blesses those people
who are treated badly for doing right.
They belong to the kingdom of heaven.

God will bless you when people insult you, mistreat you, and tell all kinds of evil lies about you because of me. Be happy and excited! You will have a great reward in heaven. People did these same things to the prophets who lived long ago.

# Love Your Enemies!

Luke
6.27-31

This is what I say to all who will listen to me:

Love your enemies, and be good to everyone who hates you. Ask God to bless anyone who curses you, and pray for everyone who is cruel to you. If someone slaps you on one cheek, don't stop that person from slapping you on the other cheek. If someone wants to take your coat, don't try to keep back your shirt. Give to everyone who asks and don't ask people to return what they have taken from you. Treat others just as you want to be treated.

# Ask and You Shall Receive

Matthew
7.7,8

Ask, and you will receive. Search, and you will find. Knock, and the door will be opened for you. Everyone who asks will receive. Everyone who searches will find. And the door will be opened for everyone who knocks.

# The Lord's Prayer

Matthew
6.7-13

When you pray, don't talk on and on as people do who don't know God. They think God likes to hear long prayers. Don't be like them. Your Father knows what you need before you ask.

You should pray like this:
Our Father in heaven,
help us to honor
   your name.
Come and set up
   your kingdom,
so that everyone on earth
   will obey you,
as you are obeyed
   in heaven.
Give us our food for today.
Forgive us for doing wrong,
   as we forgive others.
Keep us from being tempted
   and protect us from evil.

## Do Not Worry!

Matthew
6.25-34

I tell you not to worry about your life. Don't worry about having something to eat, drink, or wear. Isn't life more than food or clothing? Look at the birds in the sky! They don't plant or harvest. They don't even store grain in barns. Yet your Father in heaven takes care of them. Aren't you worth more than birds?

Can worry make you live longer? Why worry about clothes? Look how the wild flowers grow. They don't work hard to make their clothes. But I tell you that Solomon with all his wealth wasn't as well clothed as one of them. God gives such beauty to everything that grows in the fields, even though it is here today and thrown into a fire tomorrow. He will surely do even more for you! Why do you have such little faith?

Don't worry and ask yourselves, "Will we have anything to eat? Will we have anything to drink? Will we have any clothes to wear?" Only people who don't know God are always worrying about such things. Your Father in heaven knows that you need all of these. But more than anything else, put God's work first and do what he wants. Then the other things will be yours as well.

Don't worry about tomorrow. It will take care of itself. You have enough to worry about today.

## Two Roads

Matthew
7.13,14

Go in through the narrow gate. The gate to destruction is wide, and the road that leads there is easy to follow. A lot of people go through that gate. But the gate to life is very narrow. The road that leads there is so hard to follow that only a few people find it.

## A House Built on Rock

Matthew
7.24-29

Anyone who hears and obeys these teachings of mine is like a wise person who built a house on solid rock. Rain poured down, rivers flooded, and winds beat against that house. But it did not fall, because it was built on solid rock.

Anyone who hears my teachings and doesn't obey them is like a foolish person who built a house on sand. The rain poured down, the rivers flooded, and the winds blew and beat against that house. Finally, it fell with a crash.

When Jesus finished speaking, the crowds were surprised at his teaching. He taught them like someone with authority, and not like their teachers of the Law of Moses.

# Jesus Helps People

## The Leper

Luke
5.12-16

Jesus came to a town where there was a man who had leprosy. When the man saw Jesus, he knelt down to the ground in front of Jesus and begged, "Lord, you have the power to make me well, if only you wanted to."

Jesus put his hand on him and said, "I want to! Now you are well." At once the man's leprosy disappeared. Jesus told him, "Don't tell anyone about this, but go and show yourself to the priest. Offer a gift to the priest, just as Moses commanded, and everyone will know that you have been healed."

News about Jesus kept spreading. Large crowds came to listen to him teach and to be healed of their diseases. But Jesus would often go to some place where he could be alone and pray.

## The Crippled Man

Luke
5.17-26

One day some Pharisees and experts in the Law of Moses sat listening to Jesus teach. They had come from every village in Galilee and Judea and from Jerusalem.

God had given Jesus the power to heal the sick, and some people came carrying a crippled man on a mat. They tried to take him inside the house and put him in front of Jesus. But because of the crowd, they could not get him to Jesus. So they went up on the roof, where they removed some tiles and let the mat down in the middle of the room.

When Jesus saw how much faith they had, he said to the crippled man, "My friend, your sins are forgiven."

The Pharisees and the experts began arguing, "Jesus must think he is God! Only God can forgive sins."

Jesus knew what they were thinking, and he said, "Why are you thinking that? Is it easier for me to tell this crippled man that his sins are forgiven or to tell him to get up and walk? But now you will see that the Son of Man has the right to forgive sins here on earth." Jesus then said to the man, "Get up! Pick up your mat and walk home."

At once the man stood up in front of everyone. He picked up his mat and went home, giving thanks to God. Everyone was amazed and praised God. What they saw surprised them, and they said, "We have seen a great miracle today!"

## An Officer in Capernaum

Luke
7.2b-10

An army officer's servant was sick and about to die. The officer liked this servant very much. And when he heard about Jesus, he sent some Jewish leaders to ask him to come and heal the servant.

The leaders went to Jesus and begged him to do something. They said, "This man deserves your help! He loves our nation and even built us a meeting place." So Jesus went with them.

When Jesus wasn't far from the house, the officer sent some friends to tell him, "Lord, don't go to any trouble for me! I am not good enough for you to come into my house. And I am certainly not worthy to come to you. Just say the word, and my servant will get well. I have officers who give orders to me, and I have soldiers who take orders from me. I can say to one of them, 'Go!' and he goes. I can say to another, 'Come!' and he comes. I can say to my servant, 'Do this!' and he will do it."

When Jesus heard this, he was so surprised that he turned and said to the crowd following him, "In all of Israel I've never found anyone with this much faith!"

The officer's friends returned and found the servant well.

## Nicodemus

John
3.1-8

There was a man named Nicodemus who was a Pharisee and a Jewish leader. One night he went to Jesus and said, "Sir, we know that God has sent you to teach us. You could not work these miracles, unless God were with you."

Jesus replied, "I tell you for certain that you must be born from above before you can see God's kingdom!"

Nicodemus asked, "How can a grown man ever be born a second time?"

Jesus answered:

I tell you for certain that before you can get into God's kingdom, you must be born not only by water, but by the Spirit. Humans give life to their children. Yet only God's Spirit can change you into a child of God. Don't be surprised when I say that you must be born from above. Only God's Spirit gives new life. The Spirit is like the wind that blows wherever it wants to. You can hear the wind, but you don't know where it comes from or where it is going.

Then Jesus taught Nicodemus to believe in him as the Son of God:

John
3.14-17

The Son of Man must be lifted up, just as that metal snake was lifted up by Moses in the desert. Then everyone who has faith in the Son of Man will have eternal life.

God loved the people of this world so much that he gave his only Son, so that everyone who has faith in him will have eternal life and never really die. God did not send his Son into the world to condemn its people. He sent him to save them!

# The Woman Caught in Adultery

Later on, Jesus was again in Jerusalem. All the people gathered around him in the temple, and he sat down and began to teach them.

John
8.3-11

The Pharisees and the teachers of the Law of Moses brought in a woman who had been caught in bed with a man who wasn't her husband. They made her stand in the middle of the crowd. Then they said, "Teacher, this woman was caught sleeping with a man who isn't her husband. The Law of Moses teaches that a woman like this should be stoned to death! What do you say?"

They asked Jesus this question, because they wanted to test him and bring some charge against him. But Jesus simply bent over and started writing on the ground with his finger.

They kept on asking Jesus about the woman. Finally, he stood up and said, "If any of you have never sinned, then go ahead and throw the first stone at her!" Once again he bent over and began writing on the ground. The people left one by one, beginning with the oldest. Finally, Jesus and the woman were there alone.

Jesus stood up and asked her, "Where is everyone? Isn't there anyone left to accuse you?"

"No sir," the woman answered.

Then Jesus told her, "I am not going to accuse you either. You may go now, but don't sin anymore."

203

# Jesus and His Disciples

## The Twelve Apostles

Luke
6.12b-16

Jesus went off to a mountain to pray, and he spent the whole night there. The next morning he called his disciples together and chose twelve of them to be his apostles. One was Simon, and Jesus named him Peter. Another was Andrew, Peter's brother. There were also James, John, Philip, Bartholomew, Matthew, Thomas, and James the son of Alphaeus. The rest of the apostles were Simon, known as the Eager One, Jude, who was the son of James, and Judas Iscariot, who later betrayed Jesus.

## Jesus Calms the Storm

Mark
4.1,35,37-41

The next time Jesus taught beside Lake Galilee, a big crowd gathered. It was so large that he had to sit in a boat out on the lake, while the people stood on the shore. . . .

That evening, Jesus said to his disciples, "Let's cross to the east side. . . ."

Suddenly a windstorm struck the lake. Waves started splashing into the boat, and it was about to sink.

Jesus was in the back of the boat with his head on a pillow, and he was asleep. His disciples woke him and said, "Teacher, don't you care that we're about to drown?"

Jesus got up and ordered the wind and the waves to be quiet. The wind stopped, and everything was calm.

Jesus asked his disciples, "Why were you afraid? Don't you have any faith?"

Now they were more afraid than ever and said to each other, "Who is this? Even the wind and the waves obey him!"

# Jesus Has Power and Shows Love

## *Jairus' Daughter*

Mark
5.22-24

One day when Jesus was again at the lakeside, a large crowd gathered around him. The person in charge of the Jewish meeting place was also there. His name was Jairus, and when he saw Jesus, he went over to him. He knelt at Jesus' feet and started begging him for help. He said, "My daughter is about to die! Please come and touch her, so she will get well and live." Jesus went with Jairus. Many people followed along and kept crowding around.

Mark
5.35b-43

Some men came from Jairus' home and said, "Your daughter has died! Why bother the teacher anymore?"

Jesus heard what they said, and he said to Jairus, "Don't worry. Just have faith!"

Jesus did not let anyone go with him except Peter and the two brothers, James and John. They went home with Jairus and saw the people crying and making a lot of noise. Then Jesus went inside and said to them, "Why are you crying and carrying on like this? The child isn't dead. She is just asleep." But the people laughed at him.

After Jesus had sent them all out of the house, he took the girl's father and mother and his three disciples and went to where she was. He took the twelve-year-old girl by the hand and said, "Talitha, koum!" which means, "Little girl, get up!" The girl got right up and started walking around.

Everyone was greatly surprised. But Jesus ordered them not to tell anyone what had happened. Then he said, "Give her something to eat."

## Jesus Raises Up a Widow's Son in Nain

Luke
7.11-17

Jesus and his disciples were on their way to the town of Nain, and a big crowd was going along with them. As they came near the gate of the town, they saw people carrying out the body of a widow's only son. Many people from the town were walking along with her.

When the Lord saw the woman, he felt sorry for her and said, "Don't cry!"

Jesus went over and touched the stretcher on which the people were carrying the dead boy. They stopped, and Jesus said, "Young man, get up!" The boy sat up and began to speak. Jesus then gave him back to his mother.

Everyone was frightened and praised God. They said, "A great prophet is here with us! God has come to his people."

News about Jesus spread all over Judea and everywhere else in that part of the country.

## A Woman Whose Sins Were Forgiven

Luke
7.36-50

A Pharisee invited Jesus to have dinner with him. So Jesus went to the Pharisee's home and got ready to eat.

When a sinful woman in that town found out that Jesus was there, she bought an expensive bottle of perfume. Then she came and stood behind Jesus. She cried and started washing his feet with her tears and drying them with her hair. The woman kissed his feet and poured the perfume on them.

The Pharisee who had invited Jesus saw this and said to himself, "If this man really were a prophet, he would know what kind of woman is touching him! He would know that she is a sinner."

Jesus said to the Pharisee, "Simon, I have something to say to you."

"Teacher, what is it?" Simon replied.

Jesus told him, "Two people were in debt to a moneylender. One of them owed him five hundred silver coins, and the other owed him fifty. Since neither of them could pay him back, the moneylender said that they didn't have to pay him anything. Which one of them will like him more?"

Simon answered, "I suppose it would be the one who had owed more and didn't have to pay it back."

"You are right," Jesus said.

He turned toward the woman and said to Simon, "Have you noticed this woman? When I came into your home, you didn't give me any water so I could wash my feet. But she has washed my feet with her tears and dried them with her hair. You didn't greet me with a kiss, but from the time I came in, she has not stopped kissing my feet. You didn't even pour olive oil on my head, but she has poured expensive perfume on my feet. So I tell you that all her sins are forgiven, and that is why she has shown great love. But anyone who has been forgiven for only a little will show only a little love."

Then Jesus said to the woman, "Your sins are forgiven."

Some other guests started saying to one another, "Who is this who dares to forgive sins?"

But Jesus told the woman, "Because of your faith, you are now saved. May God give you peace!"

## Jesus' Followers

Luke
8.1-3

Soon after this, Jesus was going through towns and villages, telling the good news about God's kingdom. His twelve apostles were with him, and so were some women who had been healed of evil spirits and all sorts of diseases. One of the women was Mary Magdalene, who once had seven demons in her. Joanna, Susanna, and many others had also used what they owned to help Jesus and his disciples. Joanna's husband Chuza was one of Herod's officials.

# Jesus Teaches on the Kingdom of God

One day, as Jesus sat down at the seaside and a large group of people gathered around him, he went into a boat and the people stood on the shore. From the boat, he taught them with stories and said:

## *The Farmer*

Matthew 13.3b-9

A farmer went out to scatter seed in a field. While the farmer was scattering the seed, some of it fell along the road and was eaten by birds. Other seeds fell on thin, rocky ground and quickly started growing because the soil wasn't very deep. But when the sun came up, the plants were scorched and dried up, because they did not have enough roots. Some other seeds fell where thornbushes grew up and choked the plants. But a few seeds did fall on good ground where the plants produced a hundred or sixty or thirty times as much as was scattered. If you have ears, pay attention!

Matthew 13.18-23

Now listen to the meaning of the story about the farmer:

The seeds that fell along the road are the people who hear the message about the kingdom, but don't understand it. Then the evil one comes and snatches the message from their hearts. The seeds that fell on rocky ground are the people who gladly hear the message and accept it right away. But they don't have deep roots, and they don't last very long. As soon as life gets hard or the message gets them in trouble, they give up.

The seeds that fell among the thornbushes are also people who hear the message. But they start worrying about the needs of this life and are fooled by the desire to get rich. So the message gets choked out, and they never produce anything. The seeds that fell on good ground are the people who hear and understand the message. They produce as much as a hundred or sixty or thirty times what was planted.

## The Mustard Seed and the Buyer of Pearls

Matthew
13.31b,32

Matthew
13.45,46

Jesus also told these stories:

The kingdom of heaven is like what happens when a farmer plants a mustard seed in a field. Although it is the smallest of all seeds, it grows larger than any garden plant and becomes a tree. Birds even come and nest on its branches.

The kingdom of heaven is like what happens when a shop owner is looking for fine pearls. After finding a very valuable one, the owner goes and sells everything in order to buy that pearl.

## Workers in a Vineyard

Matthew
20.1-16

On another occasion Jesus told his disciples this story:

As Jesus was telling what the kingdom of heaven would be like, he said:

Early one morning a man went out to hire some workers for his vineyard. After he had agreed to pay them the usual amount for a day's work, he sent them off to his vineyard.

About nine that morning, the man saw some other people standing in the market with nothing to do. He said he would pay them what was fair, if they would work in his vineyard. So they went.

At noon and again about three in the afternoon he returned to the market. And each time he made the same agreement with others who were loafing around with nothing to do.

Finally, about five in the afternoon the man went back and found some others standing there. He asked them, "Why have you been standing here all day long doing nothing?"

"Because no one has hired us," they answered. Then he told them to go work in his vineyard.

That evening the owner of the vineyard told the man in charge of the workers to call them in and give them their money. He also told the man to begin with the ones who were hired last. When the workers arrived, the ones who had been hired at five in the afternoon were given a full day's pay.

The workers who had been hired first thought they would be given more than the others. But when they were given the same, they began complaining to the owner of the vineyard. They said, "The ones who were hired last worked for only one hour. But you paid them the same that you did us. And we worked in the hot sun all day long!"

The owner answered one of them, "Friend, I didn't cheat you. I paid you exactly what we agreed on. Take your money now and go! What business is it of yours if I want to pay them the same that I paid you? Don't I have the right to do what I want with my own money? Why should you be jealous, if I want to be generous?"

Jesus then said, "So it is. Everyone who is now first will be last, and everyone who is last will be first."

# Jesus Is God's Son

## *Jesus Feeds Five Thousand*

John
6.1-15a

Jesus crossed Lake Galilee, which was also known as Lake Tiberias. A large crowd had seen him work miracles to heal the sick, and those people went with him. It was almost time for the Jewish festival of Passover, and Jesus went up on a mountain with his disciples and sat down.

When Jesus saw the large crowd coming toward him, he asked Philip, "Where will we get enough food to feed all these people?" He said this to test Philip, since he already knew what he was going to do.

Philip answered, "Don't you know that it would take almost a year's wages just to buy only a little bread for each of these people?"

Andrew, the brother of Simon Peter, was one of the disciples. He spoke up and said, "There is a boy here who has five small loaves of barley bread and two fish. But what good is that with all these people?"

The ground was covered with grass, and Jesus told his disciples to have everyone sit down. About five thousand men were in the crowd. Jesus took the bread in his hands and gave thanks to God. Then he passed the bread to the people, and he did the same with the fish, until everyone had plenty to eat.

The people ate all they wanted, and Jesus told his disciples to gather up the leftovers, so that nothing would be wasted. The disciples gathered them up and filled twelve large baskets with what was left over from the five barley loaves.

After the people had seen Jesus work this miracle, they began saying, "This must be the Prophet who is to come into the world!" Jesus realized that they would try to force him to be their king.

## *Jesus Walks on the Water*

Jesus made the disciples get into a boat and go on ahead of him to the other side of the lake. He went up on a mountain, and when evening came, he was there alone.

Matthew
14.24-34

By this time the boat was a long way from the shore. It was going against the wind and was being tossed around by the waves. A little while before morning, Jesus came walking on the water toward his disciples. When they saw him, they thought he was a ghost. They were terrified and started screaming.

At once, Jesus said to them, "Don't worry! I am Jesus. Don't be afraid."

Peter replied, "Lord, if it is really you, tell me to come to you on the water."

"Come on!" Jesus said. Peter then got out of the boat and started walking on the water toward him.

But when Peter saw how strong the wind was, he was afraid and started sinking. "Save me, Lord!" he shouted.

Right away, Jesus reached out his hand. He helped Peter up and said, "You surely don't have much faith. Why do you doubt?"

When Jesus and Peter got into the boat, the wind died down. The men in the boat worshiped Jesus and said, "You really are the Son of God!"

Jesus and his disciples crossed the lake and came to shore near the town of Gennesaret.

214

## Who Is Jesus?

Luke
9.18-22

When Jesus was alone praying, his disciples came to him, and he asked them, "What do people say about me?"

They answered, "Some say that you are John the Baptist or Elijah or a prophet from long ago who has come back to life."

Jesus then asked them, "But who do you say I am?"

Peter answered, "You are the Messiah sent from God."

Jesus strictly warned his disciples not to tell anyone about this.

Jesus told his disciples, "The nation's leaders, the chief priests, and the teachers of the Law of Moses will make the Son of Man suffer terribly. They will reject him and kill him, but three days later he will rise to life."

## To Follow Jesus

Luke
9.23-26

Then Jesus said to all the people:

If any of you want to be my followers, you must forget about yourself. You must take up your cross each day and follow me. If you want to save your life, you will destroy it. But if you give up your life for me, you will save it. What will you gain, if you own the whole world but destroy yourself or waste your life? If you are ashamed of me and my message, the Son of Man will be ashamed of you when he comes in his glory and in the glory of his Father and the holy angels.

## The True Glory of Jesus

Matthew
17.1-9

Six days later Jesus took Peter and the brothers James and John with him. They went up on a very high mountain where they could be alone. There in front of the disciples, Jesus was completely changed. His face was shining like the sun, and his clothes became white as light.

All at once Moses and Elijah were there talking with Jesus. So Peter said to him, "Lord, it is good for us to be here! Let us make three shelters, one for you, one for Moses, and one for Elijah."

While Peter was still speaking, the shadow of a bright cloud passed over them. From the cloud a voice said, "This is my own dear

Son, and I am pleased with him. Listen to what he says!" When the disciples heard the voice, they were so afraid that they fell flat on the ground. But Jesus came over and touched them. He said, "Get up and don't be afraid!" When they opened their eyes, they saw only Jesus.

On their way down from the mountain, Jesus warned his disciples not to tell anyone what they had seen until after the Son of Man had been raised from death.

## Who Is the Greatest?

Mark
9.33-37

Jesus and his disciples went to his home in Capernaum. After they were inside the house, Jesus asked them, "What were you arguing about along the way?" They had been arguing about which one of them was the greatest, and so they did not answer.

After Jesus sat down and told the twelve disciples to gather around him, he said, "If you want the place of honor, you must become a slave and serve others!"

Then Jesus had a child stand near him. He put his arm around the child and said, "When you welcome even a child because of me, you welcome me. And when you welcome me, you welcome the one who sent me."

## Jesus and Children

Mark
10.13-16

Some people brought their children to Jesus so that he could bless them by placing his hands on them. But his disciples told the people to stop bothering him.

When Jesus saw this, he became angry and said, "Let the children come to me! Don't try to stop them. People who are like these little children belong to the kingdom of God. I promise you that you cannot get into God's kingdom, unless you accept it the way a child does." Then Jesus took the children in his arms and blessed them by placing his hands on them.

## Jesus and the Rich Man

Mark
10.17-27

As Jesus was walking down a road, a man ran up to him. He knelt down, and asked, "Good teacher, what can I do to have eternal life?"

Jesus replied, "Why do you call me good? Only God is good. You know the commandments. 'Do not murder. Be faithful in marriage. Do not steal. Do not tell lies about others. Do not cheat. Respect your father and mother.' "

The man answered, "Teacher, I have obeyed all these commandments since I was a young man."

Jesus looked closely at the man. He liked him and said, "There's one thing you still need to do. Go sell everything you own. Give the money to the poor, and you will have riches in heaven. Then come with me."

When the man heard Jesus say this, he went away gloomy and sad because he was very rich.

Jesus looked around and said to his disciples, "It's hard for rich people to get into God's kingdom!" The disciples were shocked to hear this. So Jesus told them again, "It's terribly hard to get into God's kingdom! In fact, it's easier for a camel to go through the eye of a needle than for a rich person to get into God's kingdom."

Jesus' disciples were even more amazed. They asked each other, "How can anyone ever be saved?"

Jesus looked at them and said, "There are some things that people cannot do, but God can do anything."

218

# What God Expects of Us

## *The Unforgiving Servant*

Matthew
18.21-35

Peter came up to the Lord and asked, "How many times should I forgive someone who does something wrong to me? Is seven times enough?"

Jesus answered:

Not just seven times, but seventy-seven times! This story will show you what the kingdom of heaven is like:

One day a king decided to call in his officials and ask them to give an account of what they owed him. As he was doing this, one official was brought in who owed him fifty million silver coins. But he didn't have any money to pay what he owed. The king ordered him to be sold, along with his wife and children and all he owned, in order to pay the debt.

The official got down on his knees and began begging, "Have pity on me, and I will pay you every cent I owe!" The king felt sorry for him and let him go free. He even told the official that he did not have to pay back the money.

As the official was leaving, he happened to meet another official, who owed him a hundred silver coins. So he grabbed the man by the throat. He started choking him and said, "Pay me what you owe!"

The man got down on his knees and began begging, "Have pity on me, and I will pay you back." But the first official refused to have pity. Instead, he went and had the other official put in jail until he could pay what he owed.

When some other officials found out what had happened, they felt sorry for the man who had been put in jail. Then they told the king what had happened. The king called the first official back in and said, "You're an evil man! When you begged for mercy, I said you did not have to pay back a cent. Don't you think you should show pity to someone else, as I did to you?"

The king was so angry that he ordered the official to be tortured until he could pay back everything he owed. That is how my Father in heaven will treat you, if you don't forgive each of my followers with all your heart.

## The Good Samaritan

Luke
10.25-37

An expert in the Law of Moses stood up and asked Jesus a question to see what he would say. "Teacher," he asked, "what must I do to have eternal life?"

Jesus answered, "What is written in the Scriptures? How do you understand them?"

The man replied, "The Scriptures say, 'Love the Lord your God with all your heart, soul, strength, and mind.' They also say, 'Love your neighbors as much as you love yourself.' "

Jesus said, "You have given the right answer. If you do this, you will have eternal life."

But the man wanted to show that he knew what he was talking about. So he asked Jesus, "Who are my neighbors?"

Jesus replied:

As a man was going down from Jerusalem to Jericho, robbers attacked him and grabbed everything he had. They beat him up and ran off, leaving him half dead.

A priest happened to be going down the same road. But when he saw the man, he walked by on the other side. Later a temple helper came to the same place. But when he saw the man who had been beaten up, he also went by on the other side.

A man from Samaria then came traveling along that road. When he saw the man, he felt sorry for him and went over to him. He treated his wounds with olive oil and wine and bandaged them. Then he put him on his own donkey and took him to an inn, where he took care of him. The next morning he gave the innkeeper two silver coins and said, "Please take care of the man. If you spend more than this on him, I will pay you when I return."

Then Jesus asked, "Which one of these three people was a real neighbor to the man who was beaten up by robbers?"

The teacher answered, "The one who showed pity."
Jesus said, "Go and do the same!"

## Jesus Visits Martha and Mary

Luke
10.38-42

The Lord and his disciples were traveling along and came to a village. When they got there, a woman named Martha welcomed him
into her home. She had a sister named Mary, who sat down in front
of the Lord and was listening to what he said. Martha was worried
about all that had to be done. Finally, she went to Jesus and said,
"Lord, doesn't it bother you that my sister has left me to do all the
work by myself? Tell her to come and help me!"

The Lord answered, "Martha, Martha! You are worried and upset about so many things, but only one thing is necessary. Mary has
chosen what is best, and it will not be taken away from her."

## The Rich Fool

Luke
12.13-21

A man in a crowd said to Jesus, "Teacher, tell my brother to give me
my share of what our father left us when he died."

Jesus answered, "Who gave me the right to settle arguments between you and your brother?"

Then he said to the crowd, "Don't be greedy! Owning a lot of
things won't make your life safe."

So Jesus told them this story:

A rich man's farm produced a big crop, and he said to himself, "What can I do? I don't have a place large enough to store everything."

Later, he said, "Now I know what I'll do. I'll tear down my barns and build bigger ones, where I can store all my grain and other goods. Then I'll say to myself, 'You have stored up enough good things to last for years to come. Live it up! Eat, drink, and enjoy yourself.' "

But God said to him, "You fool! Tonight you will die. Then who will get what you have stored up?"

"This is what happens to people who store up everything for themselves, but are poor in the sight of God."

## *The Pharisee and the Tax Collector*

Luke
18.9-14

Jesus told a story to some people who thought they were better than others and who looked down on everyone else:

Two men went into the temple to pray. One was a Pharisee and the other a tax collector. The Pharisee stood over by himself and prayed, "God, I thank you that I am not greedy, dishonest, and unfaithful in marriage like other people. And I am really glad that I am not like that tax collector over there. I go without eating for two days a week, and I give you one tenth of all I earn."

The tax collector stood off at a distance and did not think he was good enough even to look up toward heaven. He was so sorry for what he had done that he pounded his chest and prayed, "God, have pity on me! I am such a sinner."

Then Jesus said, "When the two men went home, it was the tax collector and not the Pharisee who was pleasing to God. If you put yourself above others, you will be put down. But if you humble yourself, you will be honored."

222

# Who Enters the Kingdom of God?

## The Great Feast

One day when Jesus was visiting a leading Pharisee, he told this story:

Luke
14.16b-24

A man once gave a great banquet and invited a lot of guests. When the banquet was ready, he sent a servant to tell the guests, "Everything is ready! Please come."

One guest after another started making excuses. The first one said, "I bought some land, and I've got to look it over. Please excuse me."

Another guest said, "I bought five teams of oxen, and I need to try them out. Please excuse me."

Still another guest said, "I have just gotten married, and I can't be there."

The servant told his master what happened, and the master became so angry that he said, "Go as fast as you can to every street and alley in town! Bring in everyone who is poor or crippled or blind or lame."

When the servant returned, he said, "Master, I've done what you told me, and there is still plenty of room for more people."

His master then told him, "Go out along the back roads and fence rows and make people come in, so that my house will be full. Not one of the guests I first invited will get even a bite of my food!"

## A Sheep and a Coin Lost and Found

Luke
15.1-10

Tax collectors and sinners were all crowding around to listen to Jesus. So the Pharisees and the teachers of the Law of Moses started grumbling, "This man is friendly with sinners. He even eats with them."

Then Jesus told them this story:

If any of you has a hundred sheep, and one of them gets lost, what will you do? Won't you leave the ninety-nine in the field and go look for the lost sheep until you find it? And when you find it, you will be so glad that you will put it on your shoulder and carry it home. Then you will call in your friends and neighbors and say, "Let's celebrate! I've found my lost sheep."

Jesus said, "In the same way there is more happiness in heaven because of one sinner who turns to God than over ninety-nine good people who don't need to."

Jesus told the people another story:

What will a woman do if she has ten silver coins and loses one of them? Won't she light a lamp, sweep the floor, and look carefully until she finds it? Then she will call in her friends and neighbors and say, "Let's celebrate! I've found the coin I lost."

Jesus said, "In the same way God's angels are happy when even one person turns to him."

## *The Lost Son Is Found*

Luke
15.11-32

Jesus also told them another story:

Once a man had two sons. The younger son said to his father, "Give me my share of the property." So the father divided his property between his two sons.

Not long after that, the younger son packed up everything he owned and left for a foreign country, where he wasted all his money in wild living. He had spent everything, when a bad famine spread through that whole land. Soon he had nothing to eat.

He went to work for a man in that country, and the man sent him out to take care of his pigs. He would have been glad to eat what the pigs were eating, but no one gave him a thing.

Finally, he came to his senses and said, "My father's workers have plenty to eat, and here I am, starving to death! I will go to my father and say to him, 'Father, I have sinned against God in heaven and against you. I am no longer good enough to be called your son. Treat me like one of your workers.' "

The younger son got up and started back to his father. But when he was still a long way off, his father saw him and felt sorry for him. He ran to his son and hugged and kissed him.

The son said, "Father, I have sinned against God in heaven and against you. I am no longer good enough to be called your son."

But his father said to the servants, "Hurry and bring the best clothes and put them on him. Give him a ring for his finger and sandals for his feet. Get the best calf and prepare it, so we can eat and celebrate. This son of mine was dead, but has now come back to life. He was lost and has now been found." And they began to celebrate.

The older son had been out in the field. But when he came near the house, he heard the music and dancing. So he called one of the servants over and asked, "What's going on here?"

The servant answered, "Your brother has come home safe and sound, and your father ordered us to kill the best calf." The older brother got so angry that he would not even go into the house.

His father came out and begged him to go in. But he said to his father, "For years I have worked for you like a slave and have always obeyed you. But you have never even given me a little goat, so that I could give a dinner for my friends. This other son of yours wasted your money on prostitutes. And now that he has come home, you ordered the best calf to be killed for a feast."

His father replied, "My son, you are always with me, and everything I have is yours. But we should be glad and celebrate! Your brother was dead, but he is now alive. He was lost and has now been found."

# On the Way to Jerusalem

## Ten Lepers Healed

Luke
17.11-19

On his way to Jerusalem, Jesus went along the border between Samaria and Galilee. As he was going into a village, ten men with leprosy came toward him. They stood at a distance and shouted, "Jesus, Master, have pity on us!"

Jesus looked at them and said, "Go show yourselves to the priests."

On their way they were healed. When one of them discovered that he was healed, he came back, shouting praises to God. He bowed down at the feet of Jesus and thanked him. The man was from the country of Samaria.

Jesus asked, "Weren't ten men healed? Where are the other nine? Why was this foreigner the only one who came back to thank God?" Then Jesus told the man, "You may get up and go. Your faith has made you well."

## Jesus Tells about His Death and Being Raised to Life

Mark
10.32-34

The disciples were confused as Jesus led them toward Jerusalem, and his other followers were afraid. Once again, Jesus took the twelve disciples aside and told them what was going to happen to him. He said:

We are now on our way to Jerusalem where the Son of Man will be handed over to the chief priests and the teachers of the Law of Moses. They will sentence him to death and hand him over to foreigners, who will make fun of him and spit on him. They will beat him and kill him. But three days later he will rise to life.

# Zaccheus

Luke
19.1-10

Jesus was going through Jericho, where a man named Zacchaeus lived. He was in charge of collecting taxes and was very rich. Jesus was heading his way, and Zacchaeus wanted to see what he was like. But Zacchaeus was a short man and could not see over the crowd. So he ran ahead and climbed up into a sycamore tree.

When Jesus got there, he looked up and said, "Zacchaeus, hurry down! I want to stay with you today." Zacchaeus hurried down and gladly welcomed Jesus.

Everyone who saw this started grumbling, "This man Zacchaeus is a sinner! And Jesus is going home to eat with him."

Later that day Zacchaeus stood up and said to the Lord, "I will give half of my property to the poor. And I will now pay back four times as much to everyone I have ever cheated."

Jesus said to Zacchaeus, "Today you and your family have been saved, because you are a true son of Abraham. The Son of Man came to look for and to save people who are lost."

# A Blind Beggar Receives His Sight

Mark
10.46-52

Jesus and his disciples went to Jericho. And as they were leaving, they were followed by a large crowd. A blind beggar by the name of Bartimaeus son of Timaeus was sitting beside the road. When he heard that it was Jesus from Nazareth, he shouted, "Jesus, Son of David, have pity on me!" Many people told the man to stop, but he shouted even louder, "Son of David, have pity on me!"

Jesus stopped and said, "Call him over!"

They called out to the blind man and said, "Don't be afraid! Come on! He is calling for you." The man threw off his coat as he jumped up and ran to Jesus.

Jesus asked, "What do you want me to do for you?"

The blind man answered, "Master, I want to see!"

Jesus told him, "You may go. Your eyes are healed because of your faith."

Right away the man could see, and he went down the road with Jesus.

## Jesus Raises Lazarus to Life

John
11.1-4

A man by the name of Lazarus was sick in the village of Bethany. He had two sisters, Mary and Martha. This was the same Mary who later poured perfume on the Lord's head and wiped his feet with her hair. The sisters sent a message to the Lord and told him that his good friend Lazarus was sick.

When Jesus heard this, he said, "His sickness won't end in death. It will bring glory to God and his Son."

John
11.17-29

When Jesus got to Bethany, he found that Lazarus had already been in the tomb four days. Bethany was only about two miles from Jerusalem, and many people had come from the city to comfort Martha and Mary because their brother had died.

When Martha heard that Jesus had arrived, she went out to meet him, but Mary stayed in the house. Martha said to Jesus, "Lord, if you had been here, my brother would not have died. Yet even now I know that God will do anything you ask."

Jesus told her, "Your brother will live again!"

Martha answered, "I know that he will be raised to life on the last day, when all the dead are raised."

Jesus then said, "I am the one who raises the dead to life! Everyone who has faith in me will live, even if they die. And everyone who lives because of faith in me will never really die. Do you believe this?"

"Yes, Lord!" she replied. "I believe that you are Christ, the Son of God. You are the one we hoped would come into the world."

After Martha said this, she went and privately said to her sister Mary, "The Teacher is here, and he wants to see you." As soon as Mary heard this, she got up and went out to Jesus.

John
11.31-44

Many people had come to comfort Mary, and when they saw her quickly leave the house, they thought she was going out to the tomb to cry. So they followed her.

Mary went to where Jesus was. Then as soon as she saw him, she knelt at his feet and said, "Lord, if you had been here, my brother would not have died."

When Jesus saw that Mary and the people with her were crying, he was terribly upset and asked, "Where have you put his body?"

They replied, "Lord, come and you will see."

229

Jesus started crying, and the people said, "See how much he loved Lazarus."

Some of them said, "He gives sight to the blind. Why couldn't he have kept Lazarus from dying?"

Jesus was still terribly upset. So he went to the tomb, which was a cave with a stone rolled against the entrance. Then he told the people to roll the stone away. But Martha said, "Lord, you know that Lazarus has been dead four days, and there will be a bad smell."

Jesus replied, "Didn't I tell you that if you had faith, you would see the glory of God?"

After the stone had been rolled aside, Jesus looked up toward heaven and prayed, "Father, I thank you for answering my prayer. I know that you always answer my prayers. But I said this, so that the people here would believe that you sent me."

When Jesus had finished praying, he shouted, "Lazarus, come out!" The man who had been dead came out. His hands and feet were wrapped with strips of burial cloth, and a cloth covered his face.

Jesus then told the people, "Untie him and let him go."

# The Last Days in Jerusalem

## *Entry into Jerusalem*

Matthew

21.1-11

When Jesus and his disciples came near Jerusalem, he went to Beth-phage on the Mount of Olives and sent two of them on ahead. He told them, "Go into the next village, where you will at once find a donkey and her colt. Untie the two donkeys and bring them to me. If anyone asks why you are doing that, just say, 'The Lord needs them.' Right away he will let you have the donkeys."

So God's promise came true, just as the prophet had said,
"Announce to the people of Jerusalem:
'Your king is coming to you!
He is humble and rides on a donkey.
He comes on the colt of a donkey.' "

The disciples left and did what Jesus had told them to do. They brought the donkey and its colt and laid some clothes on their backs. Then Jesus got on.

Many people spread clothes in the road, while others put down branches which they had cut from trees. Some people walked ahead of Jesus and others followed behind. They were all shouting,
"Hooray for the Son of David!
God bless the one who comes in the name of the Lord.
Hooray for God in heaven above!"

When Jesus came to Jerusalem, everyone in the city was excited and asked, "Who can this be?"

The crowd answered, "This is Jesus, the prophet from Nazareth in Galilee."

## Jesus Clears the Temple Area

Matthew
21.12-17

Jesus went into the temple and chased out everyone who was selling or buying. He turned over the tables of the moneychangers and the benches of the ones who were selling doves. He told them, "The Scriptures say, 'My house should be called a place of worship.' But you have turned it into a place where robbers hide."

Blind and lame people came to Jesus in the temple, and he healed them. But the chief priests and the teachers of the Law of Moses were angry when they saw his miracles and heard the children shouting praises to the Son of David. The men said to Jesus, "Don't you hear what those children are saying?"

"Yes, I do!" Jesus answered. "Don't you know that the Scriptures say, 'Children and infants will sing praises'?" Then Jesus left the city and went out to the village of Bethany, where he spent the night.

## Paying Taxes to the Emperor?

Matthew
22.15-22

The Pharisees got together and planned how they could trick Jesus into saying something wrong. They sent some of their followers and some of Herod's followers to say to him, "Teacher, we know that you are honest. You teach the truth about what God wants people to do. And you treat everyone with the same respect, no matter who they are. Tell us what you think! Should we pay taxes to the Emperor or not?"

Jesus knew their evil thoughts and said, "Why are you trying to test me? You show-offs! Let me see one of the coins used for paying taxes." They brought him a silver coin, and he asked, "Whose picture and name are on it?"

"The Emperor's," they answered.

Then Jesus told them, "Give the Emperor what belongs to him and give God what belongs to God." His answer surprised them so much that they walked away.

# The Final Judgment

Matthew
25.31-46

When the Son of Man comes in his glory with all of his angels, he will sit on his royal throne. The people of all nations will be brought before him, and he will separate them, as shepherds separate their sheep from their goats.

He will place the sheep on his right and the goats on his left. Then the king will say to those on his right, "My father has blessed you! Come and receive the kingdom that was prepared for you before the world was created. When I was hungry, you gave me something to eat, and when I was thirsty, you gave me something to drink. When I was a stranger, you welcomed me, and when I was naked, you gave me clothes to wear. When I was sick, you took care of me, and when I was in jail, you visited me."

Then the ones who pleased the Lord will ask, "When did we give you something to eat or drink? When did we welcome you as a stranger or give you clothes to wear or visit you while you were sick or in jail?"

The king will answer, "Whenever you did it for any of my people, no matter how unimportant they seemed, you did it for me."

Then the king will say to those on his left, "Get away from me! You are under God's curse. Go into the everlasting fire prepared for the devil and his angels! I was hungry, but you did not give me anything to eat, and I was thirsty, but you did not give me anything to drink. I was a stranger, but you did not welcome me, and I was naked, but you did not give me any clothes to wear. I was sick and in jail, but you did not take care of me."

Then the people will ask, "Lord, when did we fail to help you when you were hungry or thirsty or a stranger or naked or sick or in jail?"

The king will say to them, "Whenever you failed to help any of my people, no matter how unimportant they seemed, you failed to do it for me."

Then Jesus said, "Those people will be punished forever. But the ones who pleased God will have eternal life."

# Jesus Says Good-By to His Disciples

## The Plot against Jesus

Mark
14.1,2

It was now two days before Passover and the Festival of Thin Bread. The chief priests and the teachers of the Law of Moses were planning how they could sneak around and have Jesus arrested and put to death. They were saying, "We must not do it during the festival, because the people will riot."

Mark
14.10,11

Judas Iscariot was one of the twelve disciples. He went to the chief priests and offered to help them arrest Jesus. They were glad to hear this, and they promised to pay him. So Judas started looking for a good chance to betray Jesus.

## The Last Supper

Mark
14.12-16

It was the first day of the Festival of Thin Bread, and the Passover lambs were being killed. Jesus' disciples asked him, "Where do you want us to prepare the Passover meal?"

Jesus said to two of the disciples, "Go into the city, where you will meet a man carrying a jar of water. Follow him, and when he goes into a house, say to the owner, 'Our teacher wants to know if you have a room where he can eat the Passover meal with his disciples.' The owner will take you upstairs and show you a large room furnished and ready for you to use. Prepare the meal there."

The two disciples went into the city and found everything just as Jesus had told them. So they prepared the Passover meal.

Matthew
26.26-29

During the meal Jesus took some bread in his hands. He blessed the bread and broke it. Then he gave it to his disciples and said, "Take this and eat it. This is my body."

237

Jesus picked up a cup of wine and gave thanks to God. He then gave it to his disciples and said, "Take this and drink it. This is my blood, and with it God makes his agreement with you. It will be poured out, so that many people will have their sins forgiven. From now on I am not going to drink any wine, until I drink new wine with you in my Father's kingdom."

## Jesus Washes His Disciples' Feet

John
13.4-15

During the meal Jesus got up, removed his outer garment, and wrapped a towel around his waist. He put some water into a large bowl. Then he began washing his disciples' feet and drying them with the towel he was wearing.

But when he came to Simon Peter, that disciple asked, "Lord, are you going to wash my feet?"

Jesus answered, "You don't really know what I am doing, but later you will understand."

"You will never wash my feet!" Peter replied.

"If I don't wash you," Jesus told him, "you don't really belong to me."

Peter said, "Lord, don't wash just my feet. Wash my hands and my head."

Jesus answered, "People who have bathed and are clean all over need to wash just their feet. And you, my disciples, are clean, except for one of you." Jesus knew who would betray him. That is why he said, "except for one of you."

After Jesus had washed his disciples' feet and had put his outer garment back on, he sat down again. Then he said:

Do you understand what I have done? You call me your teacher and Lord, and you should, because that is who I am. And if your Lord and teacher has washed your feet, you should do the same for each other. I have set the example, and you should do for each other exactly what I have done for you.

John
13.34,35

But I am giving you a new command. You must love each other, just as I have loved you. If you love each other, everyone will know that you are my disciples.

238

## The Arrest of Jesus

Mark
14.43-50

Jesus was still speaking, when Judas the betrayer came up. He was one of the twelve disciples, and a mob of men armed with swords and clubs were with him. They had been sent by the chief priests, the nation's leaders, and the teachers of the Law of Moses. Judas had told them ahead of time, "Arrest the man I greet with a kiss. Tie him up tight and lead him away."

Judas walked right up to Jesus and said, "Teacher!" Then Judas kissed him, and the men grabbed Jesus and arrested him.

Someone standing there pulled out a sword. He struck the servant of the high priest and cut off his ear.

Jesus said to the mob, "Why do you come with swords and clubs to arrest me like a criminal? Day after day I was with you and taught in the temple, and you didn't arrest me. But what the Scriptures say must come true."

All of Jesus' disciples ran off and left him.

## Jesus before the Council

Mark
14.53-56

Jesus was led off to the high priest. Then the chief priests, the nation's leaders, and the teachers of the Law of Moses all met together. Peter had followed at a distance. And when he reached the courtyard of the high priest's house, he sat down with the guards to warm himself beside a fire.

The chief priests and the whole council tried to find someone to accuse Jesus of a crime, so they could put him to death. But they could not find anyone to accuse him. Many people did tell lies against Jesus, but they did not agree on what they said.

Mark
14.60-65

The high priest stood up in the council and asked Jesus, "Why don't you say something in your own defense? Don't you hear the charges they are making against you?" But Jesus kept quiet and did not say a word. The high priest asked him another question, "Are you the Messiah, the Son of the glorious God?"

"Yes, I am!" Jesus answered.

"Soon you will see the Son of Man
sitting at the right side of God All-Powerful,
and coming with the clouds of heaven."

## Jesus Is Nailed to a Cross

Mark
15.21-32a

Simon from Cyrene happened to be coming in from a farm, and they forced him to carry Jesus' cross. Simon was the father of Alexander and Rufus.

The soldiers took Jesus to Golgotha, which means "Place of a Skull." There they gave him some wine mixed with a drug to ease the pain, but he refused to drink it.

They nailed Jesus to a cross and gambled to see who would get his clothes. It was about nine o'clock in the morning when they nailed him to the cross. On it was a sign that told why he was nailed there. It read, "This is the King of the Jews." The soldiers also nailed two criminals on crosses, one to the right of Jesus and the other to his left.

People who passed by said terrible things about Jesus. They shook their heads and shouted, "Ha! So you're the one who claimed you could tear down the temple and build it again in three days. Save yourself and come down from the cross!"

The chief priests and the teachers of the Law of Moses also made fun of Jesus. They said to each other, "He saved others, but he can't save himself. If he is the Messiah, the king of Israel, let him come down from the cross! Then we will see and believe."

Luke
23.39-43

One of the criminals hanging there also insulted Jesus by saying, "Aren't you the Messiah? Save yourself and save us!"

But the other criminal told the first one off, "Don't you fear God? Aren't you getting the same punishment as this man? We got what was coming to us, but he didn't do anything wrong." Then he said to Jesus, "Remember me when you come into power!"

Jesus replied, "I promise that today you will be with me in paradise."

John
19.26,27

When Jesus saw his mother and his favorite disciple with her, he said to his mother, "This man is now your son." Then he said to the disciple, "She is now your mother." From then on, that disciple took her into his own home.

## Jesus Dies and Is Buried

Mark
15.33-47

About noon the sky turned dark and stayed that way until around three o'clock. Then about that time Jesus shouted, "Eloi, Eloi, lema sabachthani?" which means, "My God, my God, why have you deserted me?"

Some of the people standing there heard Jesus and said, "He is calling for Elijah." One of them ran and grabbed a sponge. After he had soaked it in wine, he put it on a stick and held it up to Jesus. He said, "Let's wait and see if Elijah will come and take him down!" Jesus shouted and then died.

At once the curtain in the temple tore in two from top to bottom.

A Roman army officer was standing in front of Jesus. When the officer saw how Jesus died, he said, "This man really was the Son of God!"

Some women were looking on from a distance. They had come with Jesus to Jerusalem. But even before this they had been his followers and had helped him while he was in Galilee. Mary Magdalene and Mary the mother of the younger James and of Joseph were two of these women. Salome was also one of them.

It was now the evening before the Sabbath, and the Jewish people were getting ready for that sacred day. A man named Joseph from Arimathea was brave enough to ask Pilate for the body of Jesus. Joseph was a highly respected member of the Jewish council, and he was also waiting for God's kingdom to come.

Pilate was surprised to hear that Jesus was already dead, and he called in the army officer to find out if Jesus had been dead very long. After the officer told him, Pilate let Joseph have Jesus' body.

Joseph bought a linen cloth and took the body down from the cross. He had it wrapped in the cloth, and he put it in a tomb that had been cut into solid rock. Then he rolled a big stone against the entrance to the tomb.

Mary Magdalene and Mary the mother of Joseph were watching and saw where the body was placed.

# Jesus Is Raised to Life

## *Pilate Places Guards at the Tomb*

Matthew
27.62-66

On the next day, which was a Sabbath, the chief priests and the Pharisees went together to Pilate. They said, "Sir, we remember what that liar said while he was still alive. He claimed that in three days he would come back from death. So please order the tomb to be carefully guarded for three days. If you don't, his disciples may come and steal his body. They will tell the people that he has been raised to life, and this last lie will be worse than the first one."

Pilate said to them, "All right, take some of your soldiers and guard the tomb as well as you know how." So they sealed it tight and placed soldiers there to guard it.

## *Women Visit the Tomb*

Matthew
28.1-10

The Sabbath was over, and it was almost daybreak on Sunday when Mary Magdalene and the other Mary went to see the tomb. Suddenly a strong earthquake struck, and the Lord's angel came down from heaven. He rolled away the stone and sat on it. The angel looked as bright as lightning, and his clothes were white as snow. The guards shook from fear and fell down, as though they were dead.

The angel said to the women, "Don't be afraid! I know you are looking for Jesus, who was nailed to a cross. He isn't here! God has raised him to life, just as Jesus said he would. Come, see the place where his body was lying. Now hurry! Tell his disciples that he has been raised to life and is on his way to Galilee. Go there, and you will see him. That is what I came to tell you."

The women were frightened and yet very happy, as they hurried from the tomb and ran to tell his disciples. Suddenly Jesus met them and greeted them. They went near him, held on to his feet, and worshiped him. Then Jesus said, "Don't be afraid! Tell my followers to go to Galilee. They will see me there."

# Jesus Appears to His Disciples

## *The Walk to Emmaus*

Luke
24.13-33a

That same day two of Jesus' disciples were going to the village of Emmaus, which was about seven miles from Jerusalem. As they were talking and thinking about what had happened, Jesus came near and started walking along beside them. But they did not know who he was.

Jesus asked them, "What were you talking about as you walked along?"

The two of them stood there looking sad and gloomy. Then the one named Cleopas asked Jesus, "Are you the only person from Jerusalem who didn't know what was happening there these last few days?"

"What do you mean?" Jesus asked.

They answered:

Those things that happened to Jesus from Nazareth. By what he did and said he showed that he was a powerful prophet, who pleased God and all the people. Then the chief priests and our leaders had him arrested and sentenced to die on a cross. We had hoped that he would be the one to set Israel free! But it has already been three days since all this happened.

Some women in our group surprised us. They had gone to the tomb early in the morning, but did not find the body of Jesus. They came back, saying that they had seen a vision of angels who told them that he is alive. Some men from our group went to the tomb and found it just as the women had said. But they didn't see Jesus either.

Then Jesus asked the two disciples, "Why can't you understand? How can you be so slow to believe all that the prophets said? Didn't you know that the Messiah would have to suffer before he was given his glory?" Jesus then explained everything written about himself in the Scriptures, beginning with the Law of Moses and the Books of the Prophets.

When the two of them came near the village where they were going, Jesus seemed to be going farther. They begged him, "Stay with us! It's already late, and the sun is going down." So Jesus went into the house to stay with them.

After Jesus sat down to eat, he took some bread. He blessed it and broke it. Then he gave it to them. At once they knew who he was, but he disappeared. They said to each other, "When he talked with us along the road and explained the Scriptures to us, didn't it warm our hearts?" So they got right up and returned to Jerusalem.

## The Disciples Gather in Jerusalem

Luke
24.33b-43

The two disciples found the eleven apostles and the others gathered together. And they learned from the group that the Lord was really alive and had appeared to Peter. Then the disciples from Emmaus told what happened on the road and how they knew he was the Lord when he broke the bread.

While Jesus' disciples were talking about what had happened, Jesus appeared and greeted them. They were frightened and terrified because they thought they were seeing a ghost.

But Jesus said, "Why are you so frightened? Why do you doubt? Look at my hands and my feet and see who I am! Touch me and find out for yourselves. Ghosts don't have flesh and bones as you see I have."

After Jesus said this, he showed them his hands and his feet. The disciples were so glad and amazed that they could not believe it. Jesus then asked them, "Do you have something to eat?" They gave him a piece of baked fish. He took it and ate it as they watched.

## Doubting Thomas

John
20.24-29

Although Thomas the Twin was one of the twelve disciples, he wasn't with the others when Jesus appeared to them. So they told him, "We have seen the Lord!"

But Thomas said, "First, I must see the nail scars in his hands and touch them with my finger. I must put my hand where the spear went into his side. I won't believe unless I do this!"

A week later the disciples were together again. This time, Thomas was with them. Jesus came in while the doors were still locked and stood in the middle of the group. He greeted his disciples and said to Thomas, "Put your finger here and look at my hands! Put your hand into my side. Stop doubting and have faith!"

Thomas replied, "You are my Lord and my God!"

Jesus said, "Thomas, do you have faith because you have seen me? The people who have faith in me without seeing me are the ones who are really blessed!"

## Jesus Appears at Lake Tiberias

John
21.1-14

Jesus later appeared to his disciples along the shore of Lake Tiberias. Simon Peter, Thomas the Twin, Nathanael from Cana in Galilee, and the brothers James and John, were there, together with two other disciples. Simon Peter said, "I'm going fishing!"

The others said, "We will go with you." They went out in their boat. But they didn't catch a thing that night.

Early the next morning Jesus stood on the shore, but the disciples did not realize who he was. Jesus shouted, "Friends, have you caught anything?"

"No!" they answered.

So he told them, "Let your net down on the right side of your boat, and you will catch some fish."

They did, and the net was so full of fish that they could not drag it up into the boat.

Jesus' favorite disciple told Peter, "It's the Lord!" When Simon heard that it was the Lord, he put on the clothes that he had taken off while he was working. Then he jumped into the water. The boat was only about a hundred yards from shore. So the other disciples stayed in the boat and dragged in the net full of fish.

When the disciples got out of the boat, they saw some bread and a charcoal fire with fish on it. Jesus told his disciples, "Bring some of the fish you just caught." Simon Peter got back into the boat and dragged the net to shore. In it were one hundred fifty-three large fish, but still the net did not rip.

Jesus said, "Come and eat!" But none of the disciples dared ask who he was. They knew he was the Lord. Jesus took the bread in his hands and gave some of it to his disciples. He did the same with the fish. This was the third time that Jesus appeared to his disciples after he was raised from death.

## The Great Commission

Matthew 28.16-20

Jesus' eleven disciples went to a mountain in Galilee, where Jesus had told them to meet him. They saw him and worshiped him, but some of them doubted.

Jesus came to them and said:

I have been given all authority in heaven and on earth! Go to the people of all nations and make them my disciples. Baptize them in the name of the Father, the Son, and the Holy Spirit, and teach them to do everything I have told you. I will be with you always, even until the end of the world.

# The First Church

## *Jesus Is Taken Up to Heaven*

Acts
1.8-14

During the forty days after he was raised from death, Jesus appeared to his disciples and taught them about God's Kingdom. One time when he was with them, he said: "The Holy Spirit will come upon you and give you power. Then you will tell everyone about me in Jerusalem, in all Judea, in Samaria, and everywhere in the world." After Jesus had said this and while they were watching, he was taken up into a cloud. They could not see him, but as he went up, they kept looking up into the sky.

Suddenly two men dressed in white clothes were standing there beside them. They said, "Why are you men from Galilee standing here and looking up into the sky? Jesus has been taken to heaven. But he will come back in the same way that you have seen him go."

The Mount of Olives was about half a mile from Jerusalem. The apostles who had gone there were Peter, John, James, Andrew, Philip, Thomas, Bartholomew, Matthew, James the son of Alphaeus, Simon, known as the Eager One, and Judas the son of James.

After the apostles returned to the city, they went upstairs to the room where they had been staying.

The apostles often met together and prayed with a single purpose in mind. The women and Mary the mother of Jesus would meet with them, and so would his brothers.

## The Pentecost

Acts
2.1-8

On the day of Pentecost all the Lord's followers were together in one place. Suddenly there was a noise from heaven like the sound of a mighty wind! It filled the house where they were meeting. Then they saw what looked like fiery tongues moving in all directions, and a tongue came and settled on each person there. The Holy Spirit took control of everyone, and they began speaking whatever languages the Spirit let them speak.

Many religious Jews from every country in the world were living in Jerusalem. And when they heard this noise, a crowd gathered. But they were surprised, because they were hearing everything in their own languages. They were excited and amazed, and said:

> Don't all these who are speaking come from Galilee? Then why do we hear them speaking our very own languages?

Acts
2.12-17

Everyone was excited and confused. Some of them even kept asking each other, "What does all this mean?"

Others made fun of the Lord's followers and said, "They are drunk."

Peter stood with the eleven apostles and spoke in a loud and clear voice to the crowd:

> Friends and everyone else living in Jerusalem, listen carefully to what I have to say! You are wrong to think that these people are drunk. After all, it is only nine o'clock in the morning. But this is what God had the prophet Joel say,
> "When the last days come,
> I will give my Spirit
>     to everyone.

Your sons and daughters
  will prophesy.
Your young men
  will see visions,
and your old men
  will have dreams.

Acts
2.22-24
Now, listen to what I have to say about Jesus from Nazareth. God proved that he sent Jesus to you by having him work miracles, wonders, and signs. All of you know this. God had already planned and decided that Jesus would be handed over to you. So you took him and had evil men put him to death on a cross. But God set him free from death and raised him to life. Death could not hold him in its power.

Acts
2.36-38
Everyone in Israel should then know for certain that God has made Jesus both Lord and Christ, even though you put him to death on a cross.

When the people heard this, they were very upset. They asked Peter and the other apostles, "Friends, what shall we do?"

Peter said, "Turn back to God! Be baptized in the name of Jesus Christ, so that your sins will be forgiven. Then you will be given the Holy Spirit."

Acts
2.41-47
On that day about three thousand believed his message and were baptized. They spent their time learning from the apostles, and they were like family to each other. They also broke bread and prayed together.

Everyone was amazed by the many miracles and wonders that the apostles worked. All the Lord's followers often met together, and they shared everything they had. They would sell their property and possessions and give the money to whoever needed it. Day after day they met together in the temple. They broke bread together in different homes and shared their food happily and freely, while praising God. Everyone liked them, and each day the Lord added to their group others who were being saved.

# Life in the First Church

## *Peter Heals a Lame Man*

Acts
3.1-12

The time of prayer was about three o'clock in the afternoon, and Peter and John were going into the temple. A man who had been born lame was being carried to the temple door. Each day he was placed beside this door, known as the Beautiful Gate. He sat there and begged from the people who were going in.

The man saw Peter and John entering the temple, and he asked them for money. But they looked straight at him and said, "Look up at us!"

The man stared at them and thought he was going to get something. But Peter said, "I don't have any silver or gold! But I will give you what I do have. In the name of Jesus Christ from Nazareth, get up and start walking." Peter then took him by the right hand and helped him up.

At once the man's feet and ankles became strong, and he jumped up and started walking. He went with Peter and John into the temple, walking and jumping and praising God. Everyone saw him walking around and praising God. They knew that he was the beggar who had been lying beside the Beautiful Gate, and they were completely surprised. They could not imagine what had happened to the man.

While the man kept holding on to Peter and John, the whole crowd ran to them in amazement at the place known as Solomon's Porch. Peter saw that a crowd had gathered, and he said:

Friends, why are you surprised at what has happened? Why are you staring at us? Do you think we have some power of our own? Do you think we were able to make this man walk because we are so religious?

Acts
3.16

You see this man, and you know him. He put his faith in the name of Jesus and was made strong. Faith in Jesus made this man completely well while everyone was watching.

## Peter and John before the Council

Acts
4.1-5

The apostles were still talking to the people, when some priests, the captain of the temple guard, and some Sadducees arrived. These men were angry because the apostles were teaching the people that the dead would be raised from death, just as Jesus had been raised from death. It was already late in the afternoon, and they arrested Peter and John and put them in jail for the night. But a lot of people who had heard the message believed it. So by now there were about five thousand followers of the Lord.

The next morning the leaders, the elders, and the teachers of the Law of Moses met in Jerusalem.

Acts
4.7-10

They brought in Peter and John and made them stand in the middle while they questioned them. They asked, "By what power and in whose name have you done this?"

Peter was filled with the Holy Spirit and told the nation's leaders and the elders:

You are questioning us today about a kind deed in which a crippled man was healed. But there is something we must tell you and everyone else in Israel. This man is standing here completely well because of the power of Jesus Christ from Nazareth. You put Jesus to death on a cross, but God raised him to life.

Acts
4.12-21

Only Jesus has the power to save! His name is the only one in all the world that can save anyone.

The officials were amazed to see how brave Peter and John were, and they knew that these two apostles were only ordinary men and not well educated. The officials were certain that these men had been with Jesus. But they could not deny what had happened. The man who had been healed was standing there with the apostles.

The officials commanded them to leave the council room. Then the officials said to each other, "What can we do with these men? Everyone in Jerusalem knows about this miracle, and we cannot say it didn't happen. But to keep this thing from spreading, we will warn them never again to speak to anyone about the name of Jesus." So they called the two apostles back in and told them that they must never, for any reason, teach anything about the name of Jesus.

Peter and John answered, "Do you think God wants us to obey you or to obey him? We cannot keep quiet about what we have seen and heard."

The officials could not find any reason to punish Peter and John. So they threatened them and let them go.

Many miracles and wonders were being performed among the people by the apostles, and many sick people were healed. More and more people, who believed in the Lord, were added to the group, both men and women. The apostles appointed leaders for the church, and the first one chosen was a man named Stephen.

## The Stoning of Stephen

Acts
6.8

God gave Stephen the power to work great miracles and wonders among the people.

Acts
6.9b-15

They started arguing with Stephen. Some others from Cilicia and Asia also argued with him. But they were no match for Stephen, who spoke with the great wisdom that the Spirit gave him. So they talked some men into saying, "We heard Stephen say terrible things against Moses and God!"

They turned the people and their leaders and the teachers of the Law of Moses against Stephen. Then they all grabbed Stephen and dragged him in front of the council.

Some men agreed to tell lies about Stephen, and they said, "This man keeps on saying terrible things about this holy temple and the Law of Moses. We have heard him claim that Jesus from Nazareth will destroy this place and change the customs that Moses gave us." Then all the council members stared at Stephen. They saw that his face looked like the face of an angel.

Acts
7.1

The high priest asked Stephen, "Are they telling the truth about you?"

Stephen answered by reminding them how, all through history, God had helped the people of Israel, but they had not obeyed him. Stephen also pointed out how they had persecuted and killed many of the prophets God had sent to them.

When the council members heard Stephen's speech, they were angry and furious. But Stephen was filled with the Holy Spirit. He looked toward heaven, where he saw our glorious God and Jesus standing at his right side. Then Stephen said, "I see heaven open and the Son of Man standing at the right side of God!"

The council members shouted and covered their ears. At once they all attacked Stephen and dragged him out of the city. Then they started throwing stones at him. The men who had brought charges against him put their coats at the feet of a young man named Saul.

As Stephen was being stoned to death, he called out, "Lord Jesus, please welcome me!" He knelt down and shouted, "Lord, don't blame them for what they have done." Then he died.

Saul approved the stoning of Stephen. Some faithful followers of the Lord buried Stephen and mourned very much for him.

## The Church Is Persecuted

At that time the church in Jerusalem suffered terribly. All of the Lord's followers, except the apostles, were scattered everywhere in Judea and Samaria. Saul started making a lot of trouble for the church. He went from house to house, arresting men and women and putting them in jail.

The Lord's followers who had been scattered went from place to place, telling the good news.

# Saul Becomes a Believer

## Jesus Speaks to Saul

Acts
9.1-9

Saul kept on threatening to kill the Lord's followers. He even went to the high priest and asked for letters to the Jewish leaders in Damascus. He did this because he wanted to arrest and take to Jerusalem any man or woman who had accepted the Lord's Way. When Saul had almost reached Damascus, a bright light from heaven suddenly flashed around him. He fell to the ground and heard a voice that said, "Saul! Saul! Why are you so cruel to me?"

"Who are you?" Saul asked.

"I am Jesus," the Lord answered. "I am the one you are so cruel to. Now get up and go into the city, where you will be told what to do."

The men with Saul stood there speechless. They had heard the voice, but they had not seen anyone. Saul got up from the ground, and when he opened his eyes, he could not see a thing. Someone then led him by the hand to Damascus, and for three days he was blind and did not eat or drink.

## The Conversion of Saul

A believer named Ananias lived in Damascus. He had a vision in which the Lord told him to go and find Saul and lay hands on him so he could see again. Ananias hesitated because he had heard of all the evil Saul had done.

Acts
9.15,17-25

The Lord said to Ananias, "Go! I have chosen Saul to tell foreigners, kings, and the people of Israel about me. . . ."

Ananias left and went into the house where Saul was staying. Ananias placed his hands on him and said, "Saul, the Lord Jesus has sent me. He is the same one who appeared to you along the road. He wants you to be able to see and to be filled with the Holy Spirit."

Suddenly something like fish scales fell from Saul's eyes, and he could see. He got up and was baptized. Then he ate and felt much better.

For several days Saul stayed with the Lord's followers in Damascus. Soon he went to the Jewish meeting places and started telling people that Jesus is the Son of God. Everyone who heard Saul was amazed and said, "Isn't this the man who caused so much trouble for those people in Jerusalem who worship in the name of Jesus? Didn't he come here to arrest them and take them to the chief priests?"

Saul preached with such power that he completely confused the Jewish people in Damascus, as he tried to show them that Jesus is the Messiah.

Later some of them made plans to kill Saul, but he found out about it. He learned that they were guarding the gates of the city day and night in order to kill him. Then one night his followers let him down over the city wall in a large basket.

## *Saul and the Apostles*

Acts
9.26-31

When Saul arrived in Jerusalem, he tried to join the followers. But they were all afraid of him, because they did not believe he was a true follower. Then Barnabas helped him by taking him to the apostles. He explained how Saul had seen the Lord and how the Lord had spoken to him. Barnabas also said that when Saul was in Damascus, he had spoken bravely in the name of Jesus.

Saul moved about freely with the followers in Jerusalem and told everyone about the Lord. He was always arguing with the Jews who spoke Greek, and so they tried to kill him. But the followers found out about this and took Saul to Caesarea. From there they sent him to the city of Tarsus.

The church in Judea, Galilee, and Samaria now had a time of peace and kept on worshiping the Lord. The church became stronger, as the Holy Spirit encouraged it and helped it grow.

# Paul's First Mission Trip

Acts
13.1a,2,3 The church at Antioch had several prophets and teachers. . . . While they were worshiping the Lord and going without eating, the Holy Spirit told them, "Appoint Barnabas and Saul to do the work for which I have chosen them." Everyone prayed and went without eating for a while longer. Next, they placed their hands on Barnabas and Saul to show that they had been appointed to do this work. Then everyone sent them on their way.

Saul was also called Paul. His Jewish name was Saulus or Saul, but Paul was his Roman name.

First, Paul and Barnabas traveled to Cyprus. After they had preached the Gospel to everybody on the island, they left for Asia Minor. In one of the towns, they went to the Jewish meeting place where Paul stated that God had fulfilled his promises by sending Jesus as the Savior for Israel. Many believed in Jesus. But when some who did not believe started to make trouble for Paul and Barnabas and chase them out of the region, they left for another town. There the same thing happened. And when they were in danger of being stoned, they fled to Lystra and Derbe. There they spoke the Gospel as well.

## Paul and Barnabas in Lystra

Acts
14.8-20 In Lystra there was a man who had been born with crippled feet and had never been able to walk. The man was listening to Paul speak, when Paul saw that he had faith in Jesus and could be healed. So he looked straight at the man and shouted, "Stand up!" The man jumped up and started walking around.

When the crowd saw what Paul had done, they yelled out in the language of Lycaonia, "The gods have turned into humans and have come down to us!" The people then gave Barnabas the name Zeus, and they gave Paul the name Hermes, because he did the talking.

The temple of Zeus was near the entrance to the city. Its priest and the crowds wanted to offer a sacrifice to Barnabas and Paul. So the priest brought some bulls and flowers to the city gates. When the two apostles found out about this, they tore their clothes in horror and ran to the crowd, shouting:

Why are you doing this? We are humans just like you. Please give up all this foolishness. Turn to the living God, who made the sky, the earth, the sea, and everything in them. In times past, God let each nation go its own way. But he showed that he was there by the good things he did. God sends rain from heaven and makes your crops grow. He gives food to you and makes your hearts glad.

Even after Paul and Barnabas had said all this, they could hardly keep the people from offering a sacrifice to them.

Some Jewish leaders from Antioch and Iconium came and turned the crowds against Paul. They hit him with stones and dragged him out of the city, thinking he was dead. But when the Lord's followers gathered around Paul, he stood up and went back into the city. The next day he and Barnabas went to Derbe.

After Paul and Barnabas had traveled on, preaching the Gospel in many towns, they sailed back to Antioch.

Acts
14.27,28

After arriving in Antioch, they called the church together. They told the people what God had helped them do and how he had made it possible for the Gentiles to believe. Then they stayed there with the followers for a long time.

269

# Paul's Other Mission Trips

## Paul Is Called To Go to Macedonia

Acts
15.36
Sometime later Paul said to Barnabas, "Let's go back and visit the Lord's followers in the cities where we preached his message. Then we will know how they are doing."

After a disagreement arose between Paul and Barnabas, they went separate ways. Together with Silas, Paul traveled to some of the new churches and taught them how to live the Christian life. They continued their travels and came to the town of Troas on the west coast of Asia Minor.

Acts
16.9,10
During the night, Paul had a vision of someone from Macedonia who was standing there and begging him, "Come over to Macedonia and help us!" After Paul had seen the vision, we began looking for a way to go to Macedonia. We were sure that God had called us to preach the good news there.

Then Paul was led to Philippi. Many people became believers and Paul himself was thrown into prison. When he was freed, by a miracle, he traveled further on to Thessalonica and other towns. He preached the Gospel there as well, facing uproar once again. After this he went to Athens in Greece.

## Paul Preaches in Athens

Acts
17.16-20
While Paul was waiting in Athens, he was upset to see all the idols in the city. He went to the Jewish meeting place to speak to the Jews and to anyone who worshiped with them. Day after day he also spoke to everyone he met in the market. Some of them were Epicureans and some were Stoics, and they started arguing with him.

People were asking, "What is this know-it-all trying to say?"

Some even said, "Paul must be preaching about foreign gods! That's what he means when he talks about Jesus and about people rising from death."

They brought Paul before a council called the Areopagus, and said, "Tell us what your new teaching is all about. We have heard you say some strange things, and we want to know what you mean."

Acts
17.22-25

So Paul stood up in front of the council and said:

People of Athens, I see that you are very religious. As I was going through your city and looking at the things you worship, I found an altar with the words, "To an Unknown God." You worship this God, but you don't really know him. So I want to tell you about him. This God made the world and everything in it. He is Lord of heaven and earth, and he doesn't live in temples built by human hands. He doesn't need help from anyone. He

Acts
17.28-34

gives life, breath, and everything else to all people, . . . and he gives us the power to live, to move, and to be who we are. "We are his children," just as some of your poets have said.

Since we are God's children, we must not think that he is like an idol made out of gold or silver or stone. He isn't like anything that humans have thought up and made. In the past, God forgave all this because people did not know what they were doing. But now he says that everyone everywhere must turn to him. He has set a day when he will judge the world's people with fairness. And he has chosen the man Jesus to do the judging for him. God has given proof of this to all of us by raising Jesus from death.

As soon as the people heard Paul say that a man had been raised from death, some of them started laughing. Others said, "We will hear you talk about this some other time." When Paul left the council meeting, some of the men put their faith in the Lord and went with Paul. One of them was a council member named Dionysius. A woman named Damaris and several others also put their faith in the Lord.

From Athens Paul went to Corinth where a church had been established. From there he went back to Antioch.

Later on Paul left for his third mission trip, and then he went further on to Jerusalem.

# Paul in Prison

Acts
21.17-20a
When we arrived in Jerusalem, the Lord's followers gladly welcomed us. Paul went with us to see James the next day, and all the church leaders were present. Paul greeted them and told how God had used him to help the Gentiles. Everyone who heard this praised God.

## Paul Is Arrested

Acts
21.27b,28
About seven days later, some of the Jewish people from Asia saw Paul in the temple. They got a large crowd together and started attacking him. They were shouting, "Friends, help us! This man goes around everywhere, saying bad things about our nation and about the Law of Moses and about this temple. He has even brought shame to this holy temple by bringing in Gentiles."

Acts
21.30-36
The whole city was in an uproar, and the people turned into a mob. They grabbed Paul and dragged him out of the temple. Then suddenly the doors were shut. The people were about to kill Paul when the Roman army commander heard that all Jerusalem was starting to riot. So he quickly took some soldiers and officers and ran to where the crowd had gathered.

As soon as the mob saw the commander and soldiers, they stopped beating Paul. The army commander went over and arrested him and had him bound with two chains. Then he tried to find out who Paul was and what he had done. Part of the crowd shouted one thing, and part of them shouted something else. But they were making so much noise that the commander could not find out a thing. Then he ordered Paul to be taken into the fortress. As they reached the steps, the crowd became so wild that the soldiers had to lift Paul up and carry him. The crowd followed and kept shouting, "Kill him! Kill him!"

Acts
21.39b,40

As the soldiers were about to take Paul into the fort, he spoke to the commander: "I am a Jew from Tarsus, an important city in Cilicia. Please let me speak to the crowd."

The commander told him he could speak, so Paul stood on the steps and motioned to the people. When they were quiet, he spoke to them in Aramaic:

Acts
22.1,2a

"My friends and leaders of our nation, listen as I explain what happened!" When the crowd heard Paul speak to them in Aramaic, they became even quieter.

Paul was telling about his life, how Jesus had spoken to him on the road to Damascus, and how he was called to preach the Gospel to the Gentiles.

Acts
22.22-29

The crowd listened until Paul said this. Then they started shouting, "Get rid of this man! He doesn't deserve to live." They kept shouting. They waved their clothes around and threw dust into the air.

The Roman commander ordered Paul to be taken into the fortress and beaten with a whip. He did this to find out why the people were screaming at Paul.

While the soldiers were tying Paul up to be beaten, he asked the officer standing there, "Is it legal to beat a Roman citizen before he has been tried in court?"

When the officer heard this, he went to the commander and said, "What are you doing? This man is a Roman citizen!"

The commander went to Paul and asked, "Tell me, are you a Roman citizen?"

"Yes," Paul answered.

The commander then said, "I paid a lot of money to become a Roman citizen."

But Paul replied, "I was born a Roman citizen."

The men who were about to beat and question Paul quickly backed off. And the commander himself was frightened when he realized that he had put a Roman citizen in chains.

## Paul before King Agrippa

Some Jewish leaders had made plans to kill Paul. When the Roman commander found out about these plans, Paul was taken, at night, to Caesarea on the Mediterranean Sea. Here he was kept a prisoner for two years. The leaders from Jerusalem had made serious charges against Paul, but he insisted that he had not broken any parts of the Jewish law, nor had he done anything against the temple or the Emperor.

The king of that region, King Agrippa, asked to hear Paul's story. So Paul was brought to meet the king. He told how he once thought it was right to oppose Jesus in every way possible. But on the way to Damascus he had seen a bright light flash from heaven and he heard a voice say, "I am Jesus! . . . I have appeared to you, because I have chosen you to be my servant. You are to tell others what you have learned about me and what I will show you later." Then Paul continued:

Acts
26.19-23

King Agrippa, I obeyed this vision from heaven. First I preached to the people in Damascus, and then I went to Jerusalem and all over Judea. Finally, I went to the Gentiles and said, "Stop sinning and turn to God! Then prove what you have done by the way you live."

That is why some men grabbed me in the temple and tried to kill me. But all this time God has helped me, and I have preached both to the rich and to the poor. I have told them only what the prophets and Moses said would happen. I told them how the Messiah would suffer and be the first to be raised from death, so that he could bring light to his own people and to the Gentiles.

Acts
26.28-32

Agrippa asked Paul, "In such a short time do you think you can talk me into being a Christian?"

Paul answered, "Whether it takes a short time or a long time, I wish you and everyone else who hears me today would become just like me! Except, of course, for these chains."

Then King Agrippa, Governor Festus, Bernice, and everyone who was with them got up. But before they left, they said, "This man isn't guilty of anything. He doesn't deserve to die or to be put in jail."

Agrippa told Festus, "Paul could have been set free, if he had not asked to be tried by the Roman Emperor."

## Paul Sails to Rome

It was now decided that Paul should go to Rome. Paul and some other prisoners were put into a ship. After having sailed a long time, a bad storm made it no longer safe to go on, so Paul gave this

Acts
27.10b,11

advice: "Men, listen to me! If we sail now, our ship and its cargo will be badly damaged, and many lives will be lost." But Julius listened to the captain of the ship and its owner, rather than to Paul.

Acts
27.18-44

The storm was so fierce that the next day the crew threw some of the ship's cargo overboard. Then on the third day, with their bare hands they threw overboard some of the ship's gear. For several days we could not see either the sun or the stars. A strong wind kept blowing, and we finally gave up all hope of being saved.

Since none of us had eaten anything for a long time, Paul stood up and told the men:

You should have listened to me! If you had stayed on in Crete, you would not have had this damage and loss. But now I beg you to cheer up, because you will be safe. Only the ship will be lost.

I belong to God, and I worship him. Last night he sent an angel to tell me, "Paul, don't be afraid! You will stand trial before the Emperor. And because of you, God will save the lives of everyone on the ship." Cheer up! I am sure that God will do exactly what he promised. But we will first be shipwrecked on some island.

For fourteen days and nights we had been blown around over the Mediterranean Sea. But about midnight the sailors realized that we were getting near land. They measured and found that the water was about one hundred twenty feet deep. A little later they measured again and found it was only about ninety feet. The sailors were afraid that we might hit some rocks, and they let down four anchors from the back of the ship. Then they prayed for daylight.

The sailors wanted to escape from the ship. So they lowered the lifeboat into the water, pretending that they were letting down an anchor from the front of the ship. But Paul said to Captain Julius and the soldiers, "If the sailors don't stay on the ship, you won't have any chance to save your lives." The soldiers then cut the ropes that held the lifeboat and let it fall into the sea.

Just before daylight Paul begged the people to eat something. He told them, "For fourteen days you have been so worried that you haven't eaten a thing. I beg you to eat something. Your lives depend on it. Do this and not one of you will be hurt."

After Paul had said this, he took a piece of bread and gave thanks to God. Then in front of everyone, he broke the bread and ate some. They all felt encouraged, and each of them ate something. There were 276 people on the ship, and after everyone had eaten, they threw the cargo of wheat into the sea to make the ship lighter.

Morning came, and the ship's crew saw a coast that they did not recognize. But they did see a cove with a beach. So they decided to try to run the ship aground on the beach. They cut the anchors loose and let them sink into the sea. At the same time they untied the ropes that were holding the rudders. Next, they raised the sail at the front of the ship and let the wind carry the ship toward the beach. But it ran aground on a sandbank. The front of the ship stuck firmly in the sand, and the rear was being smashed by the force of the waves.

The soldiers decided to kill the prisoners to keep them from swimming away and escaping. But Captain Julius wanted to save Paul's life, and he did not let the soldiers do what they had planned. Instead, he ordered everyone who could swim to dive into the water and head for shore. Then he told the others to hold on to planks of wood or parts of the ship. At last, everyone safely reached shore.

The island where they landed was Malta. The natives showed them great friendliness and care. Three months later they boarded a ship for Rome.

## Paul in Rome

Acts
28.15-24

Some of the followers in Rome heard about us and came to meet us at the Market of Appius and at the Three Inns. When Paul saw them, he thanked God and was encouraged.

We arrived in Rome, and Paul was allowed to live in a house by himself with a soldier to guard him.

Three days after we got there, Paul called together some of the Jewish leaders and said:

My friends, I have never done anything to hurt our people, and I have never gone against the customs of our ancestors. But in Jerusalem I was handed over as a prisoner to the Romans. They looked into the charges against me and wanted to release me. They found that I had not done anything deserving death. The Jewish leaders disagreed, so I asked to be tried by the Emperor.

But I don't have anything to say against my own nation. I am bound by these chains because of what we people of Israel hope for. That's why I have called you here to talk about this hope of ours.

The leaders replied, "No one from Judea has written us a letter about you. And not one of them has come here to report on you or to say anything against you. But we would like to hear what you have to say. We understand that people everywhere are against this new group."

They agreed on a time to meet with Paul, and many of them came to his house. From early morning until late in the afternoon, Paul talked to them about God's kingdom. He used the Law of Moses and the Books of the Prophets to try to win them over to Jesus.

Some of the leaders agreed with what Paul said, but others did not.

Acts
28.30,31
For two years Paul stayed in a rented house and welcomed everyone who came to see him. He bravely preached about God's kingdom and taught about the Lord Jesus Christ, and no one tried to stop him.

# Paul's Letters

## *Letter to the Church in Rome*

Paul wrote several letters to the churches he knew well. He wrote also to the church in Rome, the capital of the Roman Empire. He had not yet visited the church when he wrote his letter, but he knew many who belonged to it and he wanted to visit them and preach the Gospel of Jesus to them.

### *Nothing Can Separate Us from the Love of God*

Romans
8.31b-35

If God is on our side, can anyone be against us? God did not keep back his own Son, but he gave him for us. If God did this, won't he freely give us everything else? If God says his chosen ones are acceptable to him, can anyone bring charges against them? Or can anyone condemn them? No indeed! Christ died and was raised to life, and now he is at God's right side, speaking to him for us. Can anything separate us from the love of Christ? Can trouble, suffering, and hard times, or hunger and nakedness, or danger and death?

Romans
8.38,39

I am sure that nothing can separate us from God's love—not life or death, not angels or spirits, not the present or the future, and not powers above or powers below. Nothing in all creation can separate us from God's love for us in Christ Jesus our Lord!

### *How to Live with Each Other*

Romans
12.10,11,15,
17,18,20,21

Love each other as brothers and sisters and honor others more than you do yourself. Never give up. Eagerly follow the Holy Spirit and serve the Lord. . . .

When others are happy, be happy with them, and when they are sad, be sad. . . . Don't mistreat someone who has mistreated you.

But try to earn the respect of others, and do your best to live at peace with everyone. . . .

The Scriptures say,

> "If your enemies are hungry, give them something to eat.
>> And if they are thirsty, give them something to drink.
> This will be the same as piling burning coals on their heads."

Don't let evil defeat you, but defeat evil with good.

## Letter to the Church in Corinth

Paul had visited the Greek city of Corinth during his second mission trip. Many people had become believers. Paul had heard that there were problems in the church; therefore he explained to them what faith is all about and how they should live with each other.

1 Corinthians 12.13-22

Some of us are Jews, and others are Gentiles. Some of us are slaves, and others are free. But God's Spirit baptized each of us and made us part of the body of Christ. Now we each drink from that same Spirit.

Our bodies don't have just one part. They have many parts. Suppose a foot says, "I'm not a hand, and so I'm not part of the body." Wouldn't the foot still belong to the body? Or suppose an ear says, "I'm not an eye, and so I'm not part of the body." Wouldn't the ear still belong to the body? If our bodies were only an eye, we couldn't hear a thing. And if they were only an ear, we couldn't smell a thing. But God has put all parts of our body together in the way that he decided is best.

A body isn't really a body, unless there is more than one part. It takes many parts to make a single body. That's why the eyes cannot say they don't need the hands. That's also why the head cannot say it doesn't need the feet. In fact, we cannot get along without the parts of the body that seem to be the weakest.

1 Corinthians 12.26,27

If one part of our body hurts, we hurt all over. If one part of our body is honored, the whole body will be happy.

Together you are the body of Christ. Each one of you is part of his body.

281

### Christian Love

1 Corinthians
13.4-7

Love is kind and patient,
    never jealous, boastful, proud, or rude.
Love isn't selfish or quick tempered.
    It doesn't keep a record of wrongs that others do.
Love rejoices in the truth, but not in evil.
Love is always supportive, loyal, hopeful, and trusting.

1 Corinthians
13.13

For now there are faith, hope, and love.
    But of these three, the greatest is love.

### Jesus Is Truly Risen!

1 Corinthians
15.1
1 Corinthians
15.3-8

My friends, I want you to remember the message that I preached and that you believed and trusted.

    I told you the most important part of the message exactly as it was told to me. That part is:
    Christ died for our sins, as the Scriptures say.
    He was buried, and three days later
        he was raised to life, as the Scriptures say.
    Christ appeared to Peter, then to the twelve.
    After this, he appeared
        to more than five hundred other followers.

Most of them are still alive, but some have died.
He also appeared to James,
    and then to all of the apostles.
Finally, he appeared to me, even though I am like someone who was born at the wrong time.

1 Corinthians 15.57,58 Thank God for letting our Lord Jesus Christ give us the victory!

My dear friends, stand firm and don't be shaken. Always keep busy working for the Lord. You know that everything you do for him is worthwhile.

### Run to Win!

1 Corinthians 9.24-27 You know that many runners enter a race, and only one of them wins the prize. So run to win! Athletes work hard to win a crown that cannot last, but we do it for a crown that will last forever. I don't run without a goal. And I don't box by beating my fists in the air. I keep my body under control and make it my slave, so I won't lose out after telling the good news to others.

### Show Generosity!

The believers in Jerusalem lived under difficult circumstances and they needed help from other churches. Also, the believers in Corinth were asked to take a collection for them. Paul writes about this:

1 Corinthians 16.1-4 When you collect money for God's people, I want you to do exactly what I told the churches in Galatia to do. That is, each Sunday each of you must put aside part of what you have earned. If you do this, you won't have to take up a collection when I come. Choose some followers to take the money to Jerusalem. I will send them on with the money and with letters which show that you approve of them. If you think I should go along, they can go with me.

*For the Sake of Christ*

Later on Paul wrote another letter to the church in Corinth. In it he told of how he had suffered much while preaching the Gospel of Jesus.

2 Corinthians
11.24-28

Five times the Jews gave me thirty-nine lashes with a whip. Three times the Romans beat me with a big stick, and once my enemies stoned me. I have been shipwrecked three times, and I even had to spend a night and a day in the sea. During my many travels, I have been in danger from rivers, robbers, my own people, and foreigners. My life has been in danger in cities, in deserts, at sea, and with people who only pretended to be the Lord's followers.

I have worked and struggled and spent many sleepless nights. I have gone hungry and thirsty and often had nothing to eat. I have been cold from not having enough clothes to keep me warm. Besides everything else, each day I am burdened down, worrying about all the churches.

2 Corinthians
12.8-10

Three times I begged the Lord to make this suffering go away. But he replied, "My kindness is all you need. My power is strongest when you are weak." So if Christ keeps giving me his power, I will gladly brag about how weak I am. Yes, I am glad to be weak or insulted or mistreated or to have troubles and sufferings, if it is for Christ. Because when I am weak, I am strong.

## Letter to the Church in Galatia

There were many churches in Galatia, Asia Minor. Paul wrote also to them. This is how he often started his letters:

Galatians
1.1-3

From the apostle Paul and from all the Lord's followers with me.

I was chosen to be an apostle by Jesus Christ and by God the Father, who raised him from death. No mere human chose or appointed me to this work.

To the churches in Galatia.

I pray that God the Father and our Lord Jesus Christ will be kind to you and will bless you with peace!

*Baptized in Christ*

Galatians
3.26-28

All of you are God's children because of your faith in Christ Jesus. And when you were baptized, it was as though you had put on Christ in the same way you put on new clothes. Faith in Christ Jesus is what makes each of you equal with each other, whether you are a Jew or a Greek, a slave or a free person, a man or a woman.

## Letter to the Church in Ephesus

Paul had visited Ephesus two times; the second time, he was there for two years and many became believers. Later he wrote to the church:

*Be Kind to Each Other*

Ephesians
4.32
Ephesians
6.1-4

Be kind and merciful, and forgive others, just as God forgave you because of Christ.

Children, you belong to the Lord, and you do the right thing when you obey your parents. The first commandment with a promise says, "Obey your father and your mother, and you will have a long and happy life."

Parents, don't be hard on your children. Raise them properly. Teach them and instruct them about the Lord.

*God's Full Armor*

Ephesians
6.10,11

Finally, let the mighty strength of the Lord make you strong. Put on all the armor that God gives, so you can defend yourself against the devil's tricks.

Ephesians
6.14-18

Be ready! Let the truth be like a belt around your waist, and let God's justice protect you like armor. Your desire to tell the good news about peace should be like shoes on your feet. Let your faith be like a shield, and you will be able to stop all the flaming arrows of the evil one. Let God's saving power be like a helmet, and for a sword use God's message that comes from the Spirit.

Never stop praying, especially for others. Always pray by the power of the Spirit. Stay alert and keep praying for God's people.

286

## Letter to the Church in Philippi

Paul was taken a prisoner because he preached the Gospel of Jesus. From prison he wrote to the church in Philippi. Paul knew that he would be sentenced to death and yet his letter was joyful.

Philippians 2.18b
Philippians 4.4-8

You should be glad and rejoice with me.

Always be glad because of the Lord! I will say it again: Be glad. Always be gentle with others. The Lord will soon be here. Don't worry about anything, but pray about everything. With thankful hearts offer up your prayers and requests to God. Then, because you belong to Christ Jesus, God will bless you with peace that no one can completely understand. And this peace will control the way you think and feel.

Finally, my friends, keep your minds on whatever is true, pure, right, holy, friendly, and proper. Don't ever stop thinking about what is truly worthwhile and worthy of praise.

*A Song about Jesus Christ*

Philippians
2.3-11

Don't be jealous or proud, but be humble and consider others more important than yourselves. Care about them as much as you care about yourselves and think the same way that Christ Jesus thought:

Christ was truly God.
   But he did not try to remain equal with God.
Instead he gave up everything and became a slave,
   when he became like one of us.

Christ was humble. He obeyed God
   and even died on a cross.
Then God gave Christ the highest place
   and honored his name above all others.

So at the name of Jesus everyone will bow down,
   those in heaven, on earth, and under the earth.
And to the glory of God the Father
everyone will openly agree,
   "Jesus Christ is Lord!"

# Other Letters

Besides Paul's letters, there are other letters in the New Testament. For instance, there is The Letter of James, The First Letter of Peter and The First Letter of John.

## *The Letter of James*

### *Hear the Word and Do the Word*

James
1.19-22

My dear friends, you should be quick to listen and slow to speak or to get angry. If you are angry, you cannot do any of the good things that God wants done. You must stop doing anything immoral or evil. Instead be humble and accept the message that is planted in you to save you.

Obey God's message! Don't fool yourselves by just listening to it.

### *The Rich and the Poor in the Church*

James
2.1-7

My friends, if you have faith in our glorious Lord Jesus Christ, you won't treat some people better than others. Suppose a rich person wearing fancy clothes and a gold ring comes to one of your meetings. And suppose a poor person dressed in worn-out clothes also comes. You must not give the best seat to the one in fancy clothes and tell the one who is poor to stand at the side or sit on the floor. That is the same as saying that some people are better than others, and you would be acting like a crooked judge.

My dear friends, pay attention. God has given a lot of faith to the poor people in this world. He has also promised them a share in his kingdom that he will give to everyone who loves him. You mistreat the poor. But isn't it the rich who boss you around and drag you off to court? Aren't they the ones who make fun of your Lord?

*Faith and Action*

James
2.14-17

My friends, what good is it to say you have faith, when you don't do anything to show that you really do have faith? Can that kind of faith save you? If you know someone who doesn't have any clothes or food, you shouldn't just say, "I hope all goes well for you. I hope you will be warm and have plenty to eat." What good is it to say this, unless you do something to help? Faith that doesn't lead us to do good deeds is all alone and dead!

## The First Letter of Peter

*The New Life*

1 Peter
1.3

Praise God, the Father of our Lord Jesus Christ. God is so good, and by raising Jesus from death, he has given us new life and a hope that lives on.

1 Peter
3.8,9a

Finally, all of you should agree and have concern and love for each other. You should also be kind and humble. Don't be hateful and insult people just because they are hateful and insult you. Instead, treat everyone with kindness. You are God's chosen ones, and he will bless you.

## The First Letter of John

*God's Love toward Us*

1 John
1.9

If we confess our sins to God, he can always be trusted to forgive us and take our sins away.

1 John
2.1,2

My children, I am writing this so that you won't sin. But if you do sin, Jesus Christ always does the right thing, and he will speak to the Father for us. Christ is the sacrifice that takes away our sins and the sins of all the world's people.

1 John
3.1

Think how much the Father loves us. He loves us so much that he lets us be called his children, as we truly are. But since the people of this world did not know who Christ is, they don't know who we are.

## We Shall Love Each Other

1 John
4.7-21

My dear friends, we must love each other. Love comes from God, and when we love each other, it shows that we have been given new life. We are now God's children, and we know him. God is love, and anyone who doesn't love others has never known him. God showed his love for us when he sent his only Son into the world to give us life. Real love isn't our love for God, but his love for us. God sent his Son to be the sacrifice by which our sins are forgiven. Dear friends, since God loved us this much, we must love each other.

No one has ever seen God. But if we love each other, God lives in us, and his love is truly in our hearts.

God has given us his Spirit. That is how we know that we are one with him, just as he is one with us. God sent his Son to be the Savior of the world. We saw his Son and are now telling others about him. God stays one with everyone who openly says that Jesus is the Son of God. That's how we stay one with God and are sure that God loves us.

God is love. If we keep on loving others, we will stay one in our hearts with God, and he will stay one with us. If we truly love others and live as Christ did in this world, we won't be worried about the day of judgment. A real love for others will chase those worries away. The thought of being punished is what makes us afraid. It shows that we have not really learned to love.

We love because God loved us first. But if we say we love God and don't love each other, we are liars. We cannot see God. So how can we love God, if we don't love the people we can see? The commandment that God has given us is: "Love God and love each other!"

# John Writes

Churches in Asia Minor were often persecuted because of their faith in Jesus. In a vision Jesus showed himself to John so that he would encourage the believers to remain faithful. A new age was coming and in that time they would be together with Jesus forever. Jesus said to John:

Revelation
1.17b-19

Don't be afraid! I am the first, the last, and the living one. I died, but now I am alive forevermore, and I have the keys to death and the world of the dead. Write what you have seen and what is and what will happen after these things.

## The New Heaven and the New Earth

Revelation
21.1-5

I saw a new heaven and a new earth. The first heaven and the first earth had disappeared, and so had the sea. Then I saw New Jerusalem, that holy city, coming down from God in heaven. It was like a bride dressed in her wedding gown and ready to meet her husband.

I heard a loud voice shout from the throne:

God's home is now with his people. He will live with them, and they will be his own. Yes, God will make his home among his people. He will wipe all tears from their eyes, and there will be no more death, suffering, crying, or pain. These things of the past are gone forever.

Then the one sitting on the throne said:

I am making everything new. Write down what I have said. My words are true and can be trusted.